Edward Henry Pember

The Voyage of the Phocæans, and Other Poems

With the Prometheus bound of Æschylus done into English verse

Edward Henry Pember

The Voyage of the Phocæans, and Other Poems
With the Prometheus bound of Æschylus done into English verse

ISBN/EAN: 9783744775397

Printed in Europe, USA, Canada, Australia, Japan

Cover: Foto ©Thomas Meinert / pixelio.de

More available books at **www.hansebooks.com**

THE VOYAGE OF THE PHOCÆANS
AND OTHER POEMS

WITH

THE PROMETHEUS BOUND

OF

ÆSCHYLUS

DONE INTO ENGLISH VERSE

BY

E. H. PEMBER

LONDON
PRINTED AT THE CHISWICK PRESS
FOR PRIVATE DISTRIBUTION
1895

TABLE OF CONTENTS.

	PAGE
THE VOYAGE OF THE PHOCÆANS	1
SPRING	74
NAAMAN THE SYRIAN	77
SUMMER	95
ERIPHANIS	97
AUTUMN	112
PER GLI OCCHI ALMENO NON V'È CLAUSURA	113
WINTER	119
THE PROMETHEUS BOUND	121
THE YEAR	178

824039

THE VOYAGE OF THE PHOCÆANS.

A POEM IN THREE BOOKS.

"Phocæorum
Velut profugit execrata civitas."
HOR., *Epod.*

PREFATORY.

THE citizens of Phocæa, one of the Ionian towns upon the seaboard of Asia Minor, rather than submit themselves to Persian rule, deserted their city, and sought a home among certain colonists of their own, who had founded Alalia in the island of Corsica. There is a tradition that they afterwards migrated to Helea in Lucania upon the mainland of Italy, and further, that some of them went thence to become the builders of Marseilles. But this poem treats only of their voyage to Corsica.

BOOK THE FIRST.

ARGUMENT.

THIS book shows how the Phocæans fought in vain for freedom, and then at the last, having beguiled Harpagus, the general of Cyrus, embarked for Chios; how, when the Chians refused them the gift of the islands of Ænussæ, they departed thence, and, suddenly and secretly returning to Phocæa, massacred its Persian garrison; and how thereupon, having flung a great bar of iron into the sea at their harbour's mouth, they set sail once more, vowing never to return till the sunken mass should re-appear. It then tells how they steered across the Ægean Sea, and landed upon the southern coast of Eubœa, near to Carystus, and what befell them there.

THE VOYAGE OF THE PHOCÆANS.

THROUGH stupefying depths of Space and
Time,
E'en from whose brink his baffled sense recoils,
Albeit he marks them with vain numbers, gulphs
His mind no more may fathom than his hand
That flings a stone may hurl an Alp, Man sweeps
Unconscious and unstirred ; the while, whirled on
At speed which, did she bear him without shield
To face nought ruder than her own light breath,
Would rend the streaming flesh from off his bones
And fuse him into momentary flame,
But, in the unimpeding æther-voids,
Wherethrough she carries him, encountering nought,
Is to his senses but as stillness, Earth
Rolls her set course among her consort stars.

And while she rolls, his millions flush and fade,
Speckle her broad breast for a little span,
Then wither like the lichen-scab that clothes

His crumbling temples; race o'erlieth race,
Each piling with its puny aftergrowth
Renewed entombment of the long entombed,
Till hill, and plain, and river, and the marge
Of ocean, cease to show the last faint scar
Of ruin-blurring ruin, and the note
Of record upon record dies away.

   Yet is there something of him that survives
His fate and works, and makes the dead and gone,
Of whom no wrack remains in art or mart,
In mouldering pigment or corroded stone,
Immortal through the ages; some high deeds
Are done and are forgotten, such as lack
An aspect or a quality to draw
The universal heart of changeful man
In a perennial fashion; others live
For ever through the lengthening aftertimes,
Types of their kind and standards of degree;
So stand lone peaks of deep-drowned continents,
High, unsubmerged, and rank as mountains still,
Islanded in the oceans of to-day.
That Hebrew who with godlike instinct led
His people from the slavish banks of Nile,
Baffling the Pharaoh, lives; so too in tales

That 'neath their crust of antique fable veil
Some mighty work of broad deliverance
Or wonder-breeding change, Prometheus breathes,
Alcides, Samson, Jason, Dædalus,
Theseus, and Arthur ; so Leonidas
And his Three Hundred of Thermopylæ ;
So Roman Regulus, and that firm Swiss
Who cleft the apple from his darling's brow,
Then slew their Teuton tyrant ; live all such,
From myriads of uncounted tribes and climes,
Albeit oft spurned by crude philosophy
As crazy fabrications, shadows cast
From shapes that loom through slowly gathered
    myths
Of elemental worship : none the less
Their memories the Muses shall keep green
With frequent chaplets of perennial song ;
As now, with reverent hand, nor overbold,
Hath an unworthy singer come to trace
A few stray letters on the scroll that Fame
Holds open to recall from age to age
The honours of one handful of brave men.

    Phocæa's self-devoted commonwealth ;
Her shrines disconsecrate, her Gods withdrawn ;

Homes, harbour, mart, and gardens desolate;
The warmth and light of soft Ionian life
On that fair Asian marge of midland sea
Forsaken and forsworn! Her stubborn sons,
Alone among their pliant kin, had scorned
To dwell in affluent vassalage beneath
That yoke which Persia's fire-new monarchy
Had forged for all the necks of Asia. They
Through months of wasting leaguer held their town;
Then, when all hope was ended, prayed a truce;
And while their crafty foe, not loath perchance
To rid his province of such sturdy souls,
Withdrew his host one summer day and night
An easy distance from their walls, they heaped
Their fleet with food and wealth transportable,
And ornaments and statues of their Gods,
And, old men, wives, and little ones embarked,
Set sail for neighbouring Chios; the wise Mede
Returned well-pleased to desert streets and walls,
Left there his Persian guard, and went his way.

 Bold into Chios sailed Phocæa's fleet,
But found scant welcome; well the Chians knew
Their dangerous kinsmen of the mainland; stern
Their answer to the prayer that would have reared

A peril and an eyesore on the heights
Of near Enussæ; so the exiles turned
To seek more distant fortunes over sea
Among their kin in western Corsica,
By men of old called Cyrnus; but meanwhile,
In one blind rush of passionate hate, they steered
Back on their home, surprised its drowsy guards,
And having steeped its streets in alien blood,
Embarked once more; then with a solemn pomp
Of sacrifice, deep in the waves they flung
Within their harbour mouth an iron bar,
And swore an oath which rang from ship to ship,
That never till its mass should rise again
Should desolate Phocæa see her sons.

   Yet counted they their recreants, half their host
Recoiled ere yet they started, but the rest,
A sad and stately pageant, held their way.
Behind the city broke the summer morn;
High to the east a hundred peaks, o'ertopping
Long violet mountain ranges, caught the sun;
Midway down, flowery uplands, and below,
Rich corn-clad plains and river valleys lay
Still couched in mist and shadow; still half-hid,
Long sweeping curves of sea-sand took their kiss

From the white lips of the blue Asian waves,
While from the bosom of the harbour stole
A film responsive to the breath of dawn.
In silence the long fleet with oar and sail
Stemmed the still water ; from their crowded decks
No hum of mingled voices, such as wont
To make departure garrulous, arose ;
But all sat mute, and most with downcast eyes
That cared to gaze on neither land nor sea ;
So bound them, as a spell that stayeth speech,
And sealeth tears, and holdeth eyes in thrall,
Their weariness of night-long toil, their grief,
The awe of their great purpose, and their vow.

 But, on a signal given, from every stern
Stood forth a minstrel, and forthwith a crash
Of sound from threescore harps swept through the
  line
Of ordered vessels ; timed 'twas when the sun,
Clearing the mountain heights, came forth, and flung
A full shaft o'er the waters, lighting up
Sails, hulls, and serried human visages.
A second and a third time rang the strings
In strictest prelude ; then from threescore throats,
Long-trained, melodious, as a single voice,

Pealed out their chaunt of farewell; verse by verse
It swelled and sank in solemn cadences,
Sad all the while, and as each measure ceased,
From the banked rowers, while their bodies swung
Backwards and forwards in their rhythmic toil,
Rose slowly the refrain, " Farewell, Farewell!"

  Ionia, mother of the free,
   Forgive thy sons who quit thy shore,
  Who, loving Freedom more than thee,
   Endure to call thee home no more :
      Farewell, farewell!

  Our oars are lashed, our sails are bent,
   The land-winds like our purpose blow;
  Not as our brethren gaily went,
   With us to speed them forth, we go :
      Farewell, farewell!

  For love of venture o'er the foam,
   And wealth, with blithest auguries
  They steered to find a second home
   And markets in the western seas :
      Farewell, farewell!

'Mid feast and song they launched their fleet,
   To joyous crowds their farewells gave,
'Then turned their wine-washed prows to meet
   The welcome of the dancing wave :
       Farewell, farewell !

For us no strain of festal song,
   Nor wreath nor wine for mast or prow ;
To notes of bitterness and wrong
   Our harps are tuned and stricken now :
       Farewell, farewell !

Now tyrant camps thy mountains crown,
   And tyrant horsemen scour thy plains,
Save where some sleek apostate town
   Buys ease with tribute and with chains :
       Farewell, farewell !

But not for us, oh ! not for us,
   Such barter be for life or home ;
We work no shame on thee when thus
   We set our faces to the foam :
       Farewell, farewell !

> Nor shalt thou love us less, O Land,
>   Than those thy caitiff ones who stay,
> Because we go, a weeping band,
>   To fare with Freedom as we may:
>   Farewell, farewell!

Their song ceased, but from deck to deck there
    came,
Like drops from a spent cloud, an after-shower
Of "farewell, farewell," and then all grew still;
And not a sound broke their sad silence save
The lap, lap, of quick wavelets carried by,
And creaking of dry oars within the thongs.
So turned they to the labours of their voyage;
High rose the sun, a lusty east wind bore
The great fleet on its course; then oars were
    shipped,
And fifty rowers in each company
Freed by the breeze, and glad with food and wine,
Made merry o'er their intermitted toil.
So wore the day till evening; the spent sun,
Declining in their front, left heaven and sea
To the moon's wardship; they in wearied groups
Crept under decks, or stretched themselves along

The empty benches; others lay supine
Or prone to night-skies limpid as at noon;
Sleep reigned from stem to stern, save only where
The serious helmsman sat and eyed the stars,
Or drowsy watcher at the prow or sail
Echoed his chance command; well held the wind,
And well together held the threescore ships,
Like wild-fowl keeping order on the wing,
Till the white moon, outstripping in her march
The courier breeze, grew pallid in the west,
And o'er the crisp Ægean broke the dawn.

 Then, like some mighty mass uplifted, slow,
From east to west and north to south, the mist
Night's nursing hand spreads for Earth's coverlet
Rose round, and melted heavenwards as it rose;
And where it let the sunbeams through, its wraith
Sparkled on mast and cordage, and the shields
And helms of warriors on the bulwarks strung;
Till ship on ship unveiled to left and right,
Leading or laggard, showed herself, and each
Of all their straggling conclave answered hail.
Soon as they drew together, like a wedge
Of wavering wild-geese on their leader bird,
Quick eyes from mast and prow began to catch

A gleam of jewelled points along the verge;
And cries of " Land !" went up, and shouts of joy ;
And rowers sprang to benches, and laid out
Their great oars to the aid of the slack breeze,
While women and glad children echoed " Land !"
Peak after peak, shoulder by shoulder, rose
Majestic Andros flooded in the sun ;
While, sundered by a strip of darksome sea,
Euboea to the northward soon displayed
Her diadem of mountains, lovelier
Than aught that loveliest Hellas holds for man.
Light sped the day, and ere the afternoon
Wore near to sundown all the fleet had passed
Caphareus, whose lashed reefs and ledges took
A howling vengeance for the sack of Troy,
And marble-veined Geræstus, and had reached
That roadstead where Carystus nestles safe
Within her bay, which towering Andros guards
From southern tempest, while its western side
The Attic hills protect, its east her own.
 Safe rode the well-moored fleet where pinewoods
  fringed
The inland margin of a shelving shore ;
Smoke rose from scores of fires ; a thousand hands

Wove deftly-wattled huts of leafy pine;
From stores of simple necessary food
The women furnished forth by families
Their evening meal; down sank the westering sun,
And, even as he sank, the sudden night
Gathered, and wave and pine-stem took the glare
Of reddening camp-fires; watch was duly set
Against surprise of foes, human or brute;
All sounds died down, save where some blazing
    trunk
Crackled or fell; and in a little while,
In hut, in hold, on shipboard and on shore,
Sleep spread his broad hands over weary eyes.
  But in the morning from their town, that lay
A league along the coast, Carystians came
Armed, wary, threatening, full of heat to know
Whereto this multitudinous descent
Of migrant folk upon their shores might tend.
But, fear allayed, to welcome, as of Greeks,
And those akin, they quickly turned, and brought
Presents of milk and grain and fruits and wine;
    Told them of forest glades where wild-boars
        roamed,
And meads where hares innumerable browsed,

And chestnut groves whose fruitage even then
Made mossy lawns a harvest; day by day
The chief men of the city came to learn
All that had happed in Asia, Media's fall,
The sack of Sardis, and the full-fledged swoop
Of Persia on the scared Ionian towns;
Their own stern siege, the mounds of Harpagus,
The wiles whereby they lured him from their walls,
Their flight, the Chian churls, their rash return,
Their hecatomb of slaughtered foes, their vow,
And that the first stage of their western voyage.

  Thus nightly by the camp-fires did their talk
Discursive wander; battles, markets, towns,
New temples, wondrous statues of the Gods,
Fresh forms of worship, sacred songs, and thence
To poets and the spread of poesy,
Linus, and Orpheus, Homer, Hesiod,
And all the glories of the later bards
Who sang in Epic fashion. Thus it fell
That on their eve of farewell, as they sat,
Phocæans and Carystians, at ease
On bank, and bench, and pine-trunk, by the fires
Sudden a word went round, a general hush
Spread group by group, and while all eyes and ears

Were held intent, into the midst there stept
A minstrel with his harp, and following him,
Three maidens veiled, towards whom his hand he
    waved,
One after other, naming each in turn,
Andromache, and Hecuba, and Helen;
Then to the general concourse thus began:
"Friends, comrades, old men, matrons, maidens,
    youths,
All who have learned to glory in the wars
Our grandsires waged of old through ten hard years
For Helen and for vengeance and for Troy,
Sit now and list awhile; remember ye
The great songs that our father Homer sang
Of masterful Achilles, and his ire
For loss of fair Briseis, how he left
The Greeks to fall before fell Hector's arm,
Save by his own unconquerable, and how
The gods, whose purpose none may measure, laid
Patroclus low, for whose belovèd head
Pelides, mad with grief, for vengeance flung
His olden wrath aside; and how he slew
Horse-taming Hector in fair fight, and dragged
His body, by Apollo's care kept free

From stain of outrage, round the walls of Troy;
Then to Patroclus paid all sumptuously
Funereal honours; from which hour all men
Might well say, without meed of prophecy,
' The day shall come when sacred Troy shall fall,
And Priam and the long-speared Priam's people.'
So far great Homer, but a song there is,
By some his named, for it is writ by one
Whose hand was scarce less cunning than his own,
Of Priam's visit to the Myrmidons
By Hermes led and guarded, of his prayer,
Pelides' ruth, the sad king's home-going,
Great Hector's ransom, dirge, and burial.
And for the last, if that ye care to hear,
We all are yours to tell it as we may."

THE HOME-COMING OF KING PRIAM, WITH THE
DIRGE AND BURIAL OF HECTOR.

The Minstrel.

Now Gods and chariot-driving warriors all
Lay through the night in sleep's soft fetters bound;
All save the helper Hermes; he kept watch,
Devising how he might King Priam send
Safe from the Grecian ships, unspied of all

Their wary warders; so unto the king
He went, and standing o'er him, spake to him;
" Old man, of evil little dost thou reck,
Seeing thou sleepest thus among thy foes ;
'Tis true Pelides spared thee, and 'tis true,
Though at great price, thou hast redeemed thy son ;
But threefold this thy living sons, now left
Behind in Ilion, will pay for thee,
Should Agamemnon and th'Achaian host
But come to know of thine abiding here."
So spake he, and the old man rose in fear,
And roused his herald ; then did Hermes yoke
Their mules and horses to the wain and car,
Himself, and led them lightly through the camp,
So that they passed, and no man was aware.
But when they reached the ford of that fair stream
Where Zanthus, sprung from the immortal Zeus,
Rolls ever, Hermes left them, and took way
For far Olympus, and the dawn was spread,
Robed like the crocus, over all the world.
But they with wail and lamentation drave
Their horses to the city, while the mules
Drew on the corpse ; nor did a soul meanwhile,
Man or fair-girdled woman, notice them ;

None save Cassandra, who in form wellnigh
The golden Aphrodite's equal was;
She, having mounted up to Pergamos,
Espied her father standing on his car,
And him the herald, whose proclaiming voice
The city knew; she saw too whom the mules
Bore lying on the litter, and she raised
A cry, and crying passed down all the town:
" Oh, men and women of Troy, come look on
    Hector;
If ever while he lived and came from fight
Ye joyed in him, for a great joy he was
Unto this city and to all its people!"
She spake, and straightway in the town was left
Nor man nor woman, for on all had come
The yearning of unmanageable woe;
And to the gate they hurried, thronging round
The bearers of the body; at their head
His dear wife and his reverend mother came,
Tearing their hair, and to the litter rushed,
While round about them stayed the weeping crowd.
And so would they have stayed before the gates,
Wailing for Hector through the livelong day,
Had not the old man spoken from his car:

"Give place, and let my mules come through, and take
Your fill of weeping when I get him home!"
They stood apart, and yielded at his words
A passage for the litter, and they brought
The dead man to his well-renownèd home;
And there on couch of state they laid him down,
And minstrels upon either side they ranged,
Leaders of lamentation, to whose strain
The women should in concert make their moan.
Then with her two hands clasped about the head
Of Hector the fell warrior, leading them,
White-armed Andromache began the dirge:

The First Veiled Maiden.

O young of years, my husband, hast thou died,
Leaving me widowed in these weary halls,
And this still helpless boy, whom thou and I
Ill-fated gave his birth! I cannot hope
That he shall reach his youth, for root and branch
This town must fall first, thou, its ward and watch,
Who guardedst it, its wives and little ones,
Having thus fallen! women and little ones,
Aye mount they must, and soon, the hollow ships,

And I with them; and thou, my boy, with me
Must either go, and for some pitiless lord
Slave in unseemly fashion, or some Greek
Shall hurl thee to destruction from these towers;
Some Greek whose father, brother, son mayhap,
Hector hath slain; for many a one of them
'Neath Hector's hand hath gnawed the infinite earth;
For 'twas not mild nor gentle that thy sire
Was wont to be in the rude press of arms,
Wherefore men mourn him in this city now.
O Hector, on thy parents thou hast laid
Mourning and woe accursed, but mine, mine still
The reservation of the bitterest is;
No hand came out to me from thy deathbed,
Nor had I one deep word for memory
By night and day to cherish with my tears.

The Minstrel.

So spake she weeping, and the women wailed;
Then Hecuba took up th'unbroken dirge.

The Second Veiled Maiden.

O Hector, to my heart the dearest far
Of all my children, and indeed no less,

While thou wast living, dear unto the Gods,
Who even in thy death showed care for thee.
For swift Achilles of my other sons
Sold whom he took beyond the barren sea,
At Samos, Imbros, and the iron-bound Lemnos;
But thee he slew with the long-bladed spear,
And round about the tomb of his Patroclus,
His comrade whom thou slewest, but whom thus
He could not raise again, he dragged thy corpse.
Yet dewy fresh, as one all freshly dead,
Thou liest for me in the palace here,
As though Apollo of the silver bow
Had come and quelled thee with his gentlest shafts.

The Minstrel.

Her words and tears a wail unmeasured roused.
And Helen thus a third time led the dirge.

The Third Veiled Maiden.

O Hector, to my heart the dearest far
Of all my stranger kin, for I name not
The godlike Paris, who my husband is,
And carried me to Troy, ere which how far,
Far better had I died! Already rolls

The twentieth year since from my native land
I came, yet never till this day heard I
One evil or disdainful word from thee.
Nay more, whene'er the others in these halls,
Thy brothers, or thy brothers' fair-clad wives,
Thy sisters, or thy mother, for thy father
Was ever as a father mild to me,
Would meet me with reproach, thou stayedst them
With gentle-mindedness and gentle words.
So weep I, while my heart aches, both for thee
And for my luckless self; for nowhere else
Shall I find comfort now or kindliness,
But nought save shuddering hate in all broad Troy.

The Minstrel.

So mourned she, and that boundless concourse
    groaned;
And then old Priam to his people spake:
"Go bring me wood, my Trojans, to the town,
And fear no ambush of the Argive host;
Achilles pledged them, when he let me go,
To harm us not until the twelfth day dawned."
He spake, and they their mules and oxen all
Yoked to the wains, and speedily appeared

Flocking without the city; for nine days
Of wood they gathered in an ample store;
And when the tenth light-bearing morn appeared,
Weeping they bore bold Hector from the town,
And on the lofty summit of the pile
They reared his body, and set on the fire.
And when next rose the rosy-handed dawn
The people gathered round famed Hector's pyre,
And with great floods of deep-hued wine they bathed
The embers down until they quenched the whole;
And then his kindred and his comrades all,
While from their cheeks dropped down the scalding
    tears,
Collected and anointed the white bones;
And in a golden casket these they laid,
The which they wrapped in a soft purple pall,
And in a hollow grave enclosing all,
O'erheaped it hastily with heavy stones,
To make his monument; and placed a guard
Against the well-greaved Greeks, and went their
    way.
And once again assembling in the halls
Of Priam, their divinely-nurtured king,
They held right royally a funeral feast.

Such was horse-taming Hector's burial.
  He ceased, and followed by the maidens veiled
Drew back into the shadow ; silence bred
Of awe and pity held enjoyment mute,
And reverence sealed the ready lips of praise.
Soon rose the guests and turned them citywards ;
A hundred farewells rang among the pines ;
For a brief space receding voices came
Back through the night, and died away on it,
And all the mingled stir of many folk
Seeking repose died with them ; till the moon,
The stars, white beach, and forest-girdled bay
Looked for the last time on the scattered crowd
Of sleepers, the dark fleet, and waning fires.

BOOK THE SECOND.

ARGUMENT.

THIS book tells how the voyagers, leaving Eubœa, passed through the islands to the coast of Argolis, and were thence driven by tempest to the east of Attica; how thence they steered southward, and rounding Sunium, came into the Gulph of Salamis, and so to the Corinthian Isthmus, across which with much toil and pain they dragged their ships. And further it tells how, starting from Sicyon, they passed many famous places, until they came to Leucate, whence Sappho had leaped into the sea to cure herself of her love for Phaon.

BOOK THE SECOND.

THENCE through that gusty sea which stretches down
'Twixt Ceos, Cythnos, Melos, and the Capes
Of Sunium and Trœzene, to the coasts
Of Argolis and broad Laconia,
Did they make head; there first a churlish gale,
Blowing with force malignant through the gap
That sunders Ceos from the Attic steeps,
Barred, baffled, and o'erbore them; for two days
Vainly the rowers strove, and on the third,
Blown to the northward, they were fain to seek
Haven and rest from unavailing toil;
So to Panormos steered they, on the east
Of Attica, below the blustering head
Of Cynosema, and old Brauron, where
Dwelt Artemis enshrined, from Tauris brought
By respited Orestes, when he came
With Pylades, and brought his sister home

In safety from the murderous Chersonese.
There, suffering much, with more to suffer still,
Abode they, gathering such wild sustenance
As land and sea afforded to their search,
And comforted their limbs with sleep and fire.
Thence crept they close adown the windy shores,
In contest with cross seas, until at last
They gained the screen of that protecting isle
Named Helena from her whom Paris stole,
Furtive and fateful Paris, from the halls
Of godlike Menelaus, when they two
Came thither flying from the outraged hearths
Of Sparta, and drew up their trait'rous keels,
To rest their crews, and ease her heart awhile,
And spend a summer day in dalliance.

   So by the southern headlands, round the girth
Of silver-bowelled Laurium, and the steeps
Of marble Sunium, where Poseidon sees,
Vanquished, the pillared shrine of Pallas crown
Its vaunting crest, nor only so, but far
To westward marks the victor Goddess' self
Fling forth resplendent gleams from gilded arms,
Sun-fired upon her own Acropolis,
Forced they their weary way; but as they turned

Into that gulph renowned for Salamis,
A favouring wind relieved them, till they cast
Glad anchors on an islet to the west
Of fair Ægina; barren 'twas and bare
Of folk, with scarce a mooring, but its sight
Sufficed for welcome to those weary ones
Who flung them prone in sleep upon the strand.
   Silent and sad about their brushwood fires
Sat all whom slumber had not overborne,
And weary seemed their voyage but half achieved,
And wearier than toil done, with force and hope
Failing and waning, toils that were to do.
Yet when morn rose, with shows of cheerfulness,
Put they to sea once more; the rowers sang;
And women, heavy-eyed and pale, essayed
To soothe their fretful charge; the mounting sun
Cheered their chill blood; a constant east wind
    blew;
And ere the twilight threatened them, they lay
At Schœnus on the narrow neck that joins
The Isle of Pelops unto Hellas; there
They found a waiting crowd of country folk,
And stocks of food, and stored appliances
Of ropes and rollers; men whose trade it was

To drag strange ships across the level strip
Sundering Saronic and Corinthian seas,
And save the perilous round by Malea.
There, for their ships were heavier than those wont
To use the landward ways, and toil and time
Unusual loomed for them, awhile they stayed,
And housed their wives, old men, and little ones
In hospitable Corinth, while their crews
Restored their wasted limbs, and braced their souls
With slumber and rough feasting on the shore.
Then with laborious peril did they draw
Their fleet across the Isthmus; the great hulls
With straining timbers rocked and groaned, and shook
Their corded masts, like to reluctant beasts
Who, forced from pastures that they know, o'er ways
They know not, moan and low, and shake and toss
Their horns in sullen protest, yet they go.
So at the last, but after many a 'scape,
Keel followed keel, and slid into the wave,
And one by one, refilled and manned, took way
To meet the rest at Sicyon; there, rejoined,
And overworn, once more the exiles came.

Sicyon the wealthy, Sicyon earliest home
In Greece of sculpture and her sister art
Divine of painting; chosen dwelling too
Of diverse gods, and above all of him,
Arcadian Pan, the earth-born, Hermes' son,
Rough, bearded, hornèd, hoofed, and boisterous,
Compounded man and beast and tricksy God,
Haunter of woods and hills and watersides,
Keen of wild hunting in the passes wild,
Lover of melodies and capering joy,
Gay piper to the dancing Oreads;
Reckless of godhead and his seat in heaven,
And framer only of low wiles that wrought
His frolic of the moment; fitted he
To make the God and archetype of man
Unwitting, unaspiring, uninspired,
Save by the breath of mirth and appetite.
Him long Arcadia through her flowery meads,
Forests, and mountain fastnesses adored;
Till in those later days when Livia's son
Reigned the third Cæsar in imperial Rome,
Rose that mysterious morn when brake a cry
That rang o'er high Cyllene's peak, and spread
Through every vale in Arcady; aroused

The gorges where Alpheus cleaves his way;
Swept around Corinth and her citadel;
And, shivering o'er the waters, startled all
Ætolia, and the Heliconian streams,
Parnassus, and Cithæron, and then fell
About th'astonied ears of mariners
Coasting along the fringed Echinadæ;
"Pan, Pan is dead!" the whitening ocean wailed;
"Pan dead!" the many-storied hills replied;
And "Dead, Pan dead!" in echoes died, until
The silence of a great amazement grew.

    Pan then recalling unto them encamped
Hard by his woodland shrine, one night a bard,
Who marked them spiritless about their fires,
Stood forward with his lyre. A Lesbian he
Of Mitylene, and had fled his home
For refuge at Phocæa from the pains
Of luckless homicide: a score of years
Among them, but not of them, had he dwelt,
A deathless pain that calm could but obscure,
And memories that knew not how to fade,
His constant company: yet not the less
Loved he the sturdy souls whose commonwealth
Had made his haven and his home; and they

Loved him both for his sorrows and his wrongs,
And grace of merriment and poesy
That flashed at whiles upon him, like a veil
Masking to eyes that could not pierce its film
His mutilation of the soul : so lived he
Loving, beloved, half-pitied, half-revered,
His days consuming in a maimed content
Of spiritual solitude ; so doth
Some sea-bird, whom a stranger's wanton aim
Hath left with broken pinion, live and limp
Among her plumy kin from stone to stone,
The while they swoop and soar and wheel at will
High o'er the sunny cliffs she ne'er will climb,
And waves she scarce dares venture on ; but she
May lose all sense of anguish, learn to bear
The pendent wreakage at her side, achieve
All needs of her marred life, may feed, may sleep,
Perchance grow sleek again, but never fly.

 He, being such, stepped forth into their midst,
With easy fingers struck a phrase or two
Of merry prelude, and in praise of Pan,
Ringed round by ruddy bivouacs thus began.

Hymn to Pan.

Now, Muse, the two-horned, goat-footed, boisterous
Offspring of Hermes aid me to sing awhile,
   Him whom the nymphs with songs and frolic
     Lead up the lawns of the woodland mountain.

Rocks that the wild-goat's feet never trod, they tread,
Hail him the Shepherd God of the ruddy hair,
   Sunbrown, the Lord of snowy-mantled
     Peaks and the tracks over stony ranges.

Now through the tangled thicket he wandereth,
Now skimmeth gentler breasts of the rivulet,
   Now haunteth the steeps of the hill-sides,
     Now over sentinel summits strideth.

By pass, by gorge, o'er glistering altitudes,
Keen-eyed he scoureth, hunter infallible;
   Now weary 'neath Hesper reposeth,
     Tuning his reeds to a lightsome measure.

Such none of feathered masters of minstrelsy,
Bowered under leaves through times of the flowery
     Spring,

Surpassing in wealth of sweet numbers,
   Poureth his hymns of melodious plaining.

Him hearing, clear-tongued Nymphs of the upper-
   land
Throng round the brinks of shadowy waterheads,
   They sing and they dance, while sad Echo
     Moaneth in answer about the mountain.

Now here and now there, daintily footing it,
Threading their mazes, gamesome with harmony,
   He flaunteth exultant the blood-stained
     Spoils of the lynx on his tawny shoulder.

Soft are the meads there, fragrances infinite
Breathe from the trampled saffron and hyacinth,
   That scatter their beauties unstinted,
     Prodigal, over the green-grass flooring.

Then rise the hymns in praise of the Happy Gods
On high Olympus; Him before all they praise,
   Hermes the helper, swift, unfailing
     Servitor unto the Lords of Heaven.

Who, unto watered Arcady wandering,
Roamed through the fertile mother of fleecy flocks,
  To where in Cyllene his structured
    Altar he found and a ready temple.

There he, by tender languishment overborne,
Thought it no shame, albeit a God he was,
  To follow submissive the rough-woolled
    Sheep at the will of a mortal master.

Mad for the sun-flecked ringlets of Dryope,
Toiled he, and won, and timely begot of her
  This marvel of aspect, this goat-heeled,
    Double-horned, roystering laughter-lover.

Full soon the scared nurse fled from a prodigy
So wild of look, so bearded and boisterous;
  Fled she, but his father, the helper,
    Tenderly lifted his babe, and straightway

Close-wrapt in well-furred skins of the forest hare
Bore him to Heaven, high seat of the Happy Ones,
  And proudly discovered his bantling
    Full to the gaze of the Gods assembled.

These all rejoicing, Bacchus abundantly,
Pan, Pan, salute him, Pan, as the joy of all—
—But now, my Lord Pan, having sung thee,
Must I be mindful of other measures.

The Lesbian ceased, but in their lifted eyes
And laughter lived the praises of his song;
And jests ran round, not impious, but such
As they who love and fear the Gods might dare,
Of Hermes, and of Pan among the Nymphs,
Discarded Echo and her wandering plaints,
And all that she must hover round and hear.
With cheerful hands they piled their fires anew,
Set their night watch, and on their beds of leaves
And sun-dried grasses well contented slept.
   Too weary grown for beauty did they press
With oar and sail up Corinth's land-locked sea,
Embosomed between guardian mountain-chains,
Whose emulative loveliness adorns
Phocis, Ætolia, Locris, and the heights
Of crowned Arcadia, sundering her vales
From Elis and the fertile slopes that trend
Adown Achaia to the gulph; they chose
To skirt the northern shores, evading thus

Their churlish kin of Helice, who grudged
Poseidon's image or its counterfeit
To grace in Asia his adopted home
At Panionium upon Mycale.
But these the well-earned anger of the god,
Long harboured, did with horror overwhelm,
When in the dead of night their city sank
Without a warning, suddenly engulphed
Whole in the yawning earth; sheer down they fell,
Walls, market, temples, and wide-streeted town,
And goodly girding leagues of fertile plain,
With scarce time given for ruin's shock to sound,
Or men to groan; in rode the vengeful god,
Triumphant, charioted on eager waves,
And not a wrack remained of Helice.

By Siphæ, where the good ship Argo moored
Home coming laden with the golden spoil
Of Colchis, and the spurs of Helicon,
Chief home of Phœbus and his maidens nine,
Careless they steered; nor raised a languid eye
In quest of Aganippè, or that stream,
The Fountain of the Wingèd Steed, whose foot
Struck with one stamp its prisoned waters free.
Past safely-pent Anticyra, whose walls

The Voyage of the Phocæans.

Meads of brain-soothing hellebore surround,
And past the mouth of that Crissæan bay
Wherein the deeply-nestling Cyrrha lies,
Access to Delphi and the sacred Mount
Parnassus and the springs of Castaly,
And Lycorea, where the Delphian priest
Mounted may watch the westering sun illume
Acro-Corinthus with its towered walls,
Heedless, albeit Ionians, men with hearts
All prone to loveliness and poesy,
Uncaring, with heads bent, and half-plied oars,
And sullen grown from very weariness,
Towards coveted Naupactus held they on.

Well cherished there, but ever weaker grown,
Though goaded ever towards their western goal,
Put they to sea once more; midway they steered
'Twixt Rhium and Antirrhium through the gorge,
By Chalcis and Molycria, and that plain
Well watered of Evenus, where ensconced
The town Ætolus built for Calydon
Lies girt by rocky fastnesses, and woods
That haunted were of old through many a month
By that fell Boar which ravaged all its fields,
When Æneus, niggard spurner of the gods,

Withholding seemly rites of sacrifice,
Drew down the wrath of slighted Artemis.
Them Meleager of the hero band
Of Argonautæ, hunter without peer,
Aided by fleetfoot Atalanta, freed.
To her the monster's hide in prize he gave,
Vainly; for her did Thestius' sons despoil,
His mother's brethren, whom he rashly slew;
But vexed Althea, maddened, blind at heart—
The blood-feud battling down maternity—
And minding her of ancient oracles
E'en at his birth confided, flung that torch,
Whereto her son was fated, on the hearth,
And with it smouldered all his life away.

  So by Mount Aracynthus, and those isles
That bristle like sea-urchins, named of these
Echinadæ, they sailed, and that foiled stream
Of amorous Achelous, who, disguised
In figure of a bull, essayed in arms
Invincible Alcides, by the love
Of fair Deianira thus impelled;
From him Alcmene's son, victorious, wrenched
A horn, and for perpetual emblem gave
To Ceres, stored with grain and fruit and flower;

Since when, of one branch shorn, the vanquished
    stream
Through champaigns undisturbed his minished
    floods
Rolls in meek service to th' Ionian Sea.
    Thence all outworn 'twixt Cephallenia's coasts
And Odyssean Ithaca they crept,
Slow, on a lowering wind, but moored at length
Once more, within a southern bay that turns
Securely to the east, near the lone point
Of that Leucadian headland, whence the shrine
Of Phœbus looked on those rash leaps once made
By desperate lovers for imagined ease.
There huddled round their fires in groups they sat,
Men mute, and women weeping silently;
So deep into their exiled souls had struck
Dejection of long travel born and toil.
Then, for one note of sorrow oft drives out
Its fellow, mindful of the last fond plunge
Taken so near at hand, nor long before,
By her the lovesick poetess forlorn
Of Mitylene, for whose fate and song
Men still with honour name her island home,
Stept forth their ready Lesbian guest, his lyre

Strung to a mode akin to misery;
And as they raised their half-expectant eyes,
He, to the women making chief appeal,
After some words of kindly prelude, sang.

The Death of Sappho.

Maidens, to whom love unavailing seemeth
Sprung of divine anger of Aphrodite,
Hearken how Sappho, loving, love-bewildered,
    Died to allay love.

Died, having long served, suffered, and long waited,
Lest the Great Queen, sated awhile of anguish,
Haply, twin pearls of roseate ears turning,
    Might as of old time

Mount to her car, by flying Loves and Graces
Girt, and on plumes innumerable wafted
Over proud Ocean's bosom, while the Tritons
    Wantoned around her,

Seek, as she once sought pitiful her handmaid
Drooping in Lesbos, while the sunny glories
Showered from her brows lighted as triple noontide
    Gay Mitylene.

Vain, alas, hope, sighs, sacrifice, and service
Vain; the Great Queen, seated in fruity Paphos,
Heard and not heard, watching her Nymphs with
    linked arms
        Dreamily wander,

Now beneath shade of busy myrtle alleys,
Haunted of bees and resonant of song-birds,
Now over green lawns, apple-strewn, or flushed with
        Spoils of the spent rose.

So to thy rocks, Leucadia the mournful,
Came the sweet girl-weaver of songs, whose echoes
Breathe as sweet breath of violets in spring-time
        Daintily woven.

Wasted she came, lonely and lost, her beauty
Shattered and marred, creeping along the headlands
Down to their lowest ledges lying seaward
        Full to the sunset.

Round her frail form th' immeasurable splendour
Flamed; a light air stole from the west, and back-
    wards

Fold over fold waving her white robe, softly
    Fondled her dark hair.

Thus the Winds, Skies, Ocean, the Earth her
    Mother,
Clad in combined glories of welcome, hailed her,
Calling unheard, "Come to us, O sad Daughter,
    Lo, we await thee!"

Slowly she turned, leaning against the rock-face,
Saw the white cliffs and forest meadows glowing,
Lifted her gaze once to the limpid heavens, then
    Leaped to the bright wave.

Then was there seen, e'en as she sank, a wonder!
Still, from her plunge seething, the rosy water
Sparkled and swelled and set the sea-plants
    waving,
    When in the sun's path

Rose a white bird, whiter than marble hewn on
Glistering Pentelicus, or the snow-plains
Shining in winter far above the pines on
    Holy Cithæron :

Rose, and with low flight taking wing to westward,
Voiceless it flew; and as it dipped the twofold
Trail of its plumes, brushed, as a fan, the burnished
    Face of the sleek sea.

Far and long, unflagging, the while the sun fell,
Beat its wide pinions, winnowing the twilight,
'Till in Night's hallowed haven, as a daydream
    Fadeth, it faded.

He ceased, and ceasing left them with a sense
Of suffering far deeper than their own,
They to whom love remained, and promised homes,
Though sundered from them still by lengths of sea.
And pity for the lone Æolian,
Who, chased from home and kindred, pitied them,
Not graceless in his refuge, blent in them
With sadness for that Sappho whom he sang,
Who bore more than they bore ere she would die.
For Art hath tears she mingleth with our own,
And blind and mute and lifeless though they be,
Her things of stone and canvas, words or tones

Of poesy or music, touch our hearts,
As though it were a soul that touched a soul.
So sank they into sleep, their sorrow soothed
By songs of sorrow, upon earth's wide knees,
Caressed by the still moon and tremulous stars.

BOOK THE THIRD.

ARGUMENT.

This book shows how the Phocæans, well-nigh outworn, struck across the main sea from Leucas to Sicily, and how with much peril and greater terror they passed between Scylla and Charybdis into the Tyrrhenian Sea. How, after that, a storm drove them out of their course into the neighbourhood of Helea in Lucania, where, as some say, had they known it, they might even then have found hospitality among certain of their countrymen established there. Further, it tells how, blown once more by veering winds back to the Sardinian coast, and finding themselves drifting upon a current that set southward, they despaired and would have ceased to row; but how, excited thereto by a favourite minstrel, they made a final effort, and saw at last in the dusk of morning the watch-fires of Alalia; and how they were met by the Alalian fleet when in full sight of land, and so brought their voyage to a happy close.

BOOK THE THIRD.

THROUGH starving days of hopeless lethargy
    At Leucas did they wait a favouring wind;
But, ceaselessly and chill, strong western gales
Beat o'er the isles, like some relentless flaw
Marring a system, or a fault that runs
Impassable athwart the miner's toil.
    But at the last upsprang a morn that brought
Their hour of action unto them who fain
Had culled self-pardon from necessity,
To lie supine; half-vain had been the call
To step the masts once more and lash the oars,
Till haply round the Lesbian rose a cry
That ran from mouth to mouth, "Another song,
Another song! Sing us but one more song,
One merrier than thy last, before we go!"
Sadly he smiled, as one may smile who knows
A suffering greater than the pain that pleads;
But, for he loved them well and pitied them,

So that his own lot was as nought to him,
He forthwith from his shoulder slipped his lyre,
And, wandering with meditative hand
Over the strings awhile, he sang to them
A trifle merry as his soul was sad;
A jesting tale it was of prank divine,
Culled from the stores of their Ionic Muse,
Sportive and cruel, as the manner is
Of bards, who in our later times have sung
Of merry outlaws or some freakish king;
Yet not the less he sang as one in whom
His humour blent with reverence, but who knew
How careless of man's fate a God could show;
And this in modern rhymes is what he sang.

A Lyttel Geste of Dionysus.

Of Dionysus hear a song,
   The son of far-famed Semelè,
How his will went to walk along
   The high dunes of the barren sea.

In robe of purple fine arrayed,
   His form was as a stripling fair,
Above his manly shoulders played
   The clusters of his darkling hair.

The Voyage of the Phocæans.

A tall ship cleft the wine-faced wave
    With reivers from the Tuscan bay ;
Ill-fated were the hands that drave
    Their prow ashore on that same day.

With many a nod they leapt to land ;
    They carried him aboard with glee ;
"Bind him," quoth they, "both foot and hand,
    For sure of royal race is he."

Soon brake he loose, both foot and hand,
    Nor bond nor fetter might him stay,
But hempen rope and withy band
    He snapt and flung them far away.

He sat him down among them all,
    With frolic in his eyes of blue,
Right soon then did the pilot call
    With fearsome cry to all the crew :

"What god is this, my shipmates dear,
    Ye have thus dared to take and bind ?
The ship was never built, I fear,
    Would carry cargo of his kind.

"Like to no mortal man is he,
    Olympian Halls his presence know,
Zeus or Poseidon might he be,
    Or Phœbus of the silver bow.

"Lay we no hand on him, but set
    Him free upon the gloomy shore,
Lest he grow wroth and lash and fret
    The winds and seas to wild uproar."

Then spake the captain, stern and grim,
    "See'st thou, my friend, the wind's abaft?
Clap on all sail, we'll look to him,
    Your business is to steer this craft.

"But he shall sail to Egypt's sands,
    Or Cyprus, if the wind so will,
Or to far Hyperborean lands,
    Or ports maybe more distant still;

"And at the last, I wot full well,
    He shall discourse us of his gear,
Of friends and kindred shall he tell;
    'Twas our good God that sent him here."

They stepped the mast, they bent the sail,
    Each rope and sheet they drew full taut,
The canvas bellied to the gale,
    But wondrous things ere long were wrought.

First wine, all sweet in taste and smell,
    Their fleet dark ship ran babbling o'er,
Around them scents ambrosial fell,
    And on their hearts amazement sore.

And, here a bower, and there a bower,
    A vine with plenteous bunches hung;
Aloft, with gracious fruit and flower,
    About the mast dark ivy clung.

And all the thongs and all the tholes
    With branch and tendril close were spanned;
Right eagerly those trembling souls
    Their pilot prayed to make the land.

When lo! from out the bows appeared
    A Lion roaring down the deck,
While amidships a She-bear reared
    The horrors of her shaggy neck.

Keen stood she, ravening for prey,
  From bench to bench his glances lowered;
Back to the stern the crew made way,
  And round the steadfast pilot cowered.

Then rushing forth with fang and claw
  The Lion on their captain fell;
As men in face of fate, they saw,
  And seaward leapt with fearful yell;

But, changed in shape and nature, grew
  To dolphins ere they met the wave;
The God held back the pilot true,
  And kindly words of comfort gave:

" Cheer thee, my friend," he said and smiled,
  " Much favour hast thou found with me,
Gay Bacchus I, of Zeus the child
  And fair Cadmeian Semelè."

Good minstrels all now bid thee hail,
  Thou son of comely Semelè,
For neither hand nor voice avail
  Him who would sing forgetting thee !

He ceased, and all turned merrily to work,
Hawsers were drawn, and anchors stowed, and soon,
With shows of hectic vigour, their dark fleet
Was plunging through the seas for Sicily.
There, hard by Naxos and the craggy seat
Of Tauromenium, below Etna's foot,
They landed, and with faint-eyed wonder saw
The fume of deep-impounded Typho's breath
Steam from its summit; then their minstrel told
How when the war, by Zeus for Heaven provoked,
Around Olympus raged, the Titan stood
Rearing his hundred crests, portentous, dire,
And, hissing slaughter from his monstrous jaws,
Faced all th'embattled gods, while from his eyes
Gorgon-like lights came flashing, as he stood
In act to storm the citadel of Heaven.
But him the ever-wakeful bolt of Zeus,
With thunder swooping, in a blast of flame,
Struck down astonied at the very height
Of his proud vauntings; stricken to the heart,
Charred, blasted, in his ruined strength he fell.
Now prostrate, powerless, near the Tyrrhene Sea,
Crushed 'neath the roots of Sicily he lies;
Supine he lies, in monstrous bulk outstretched

From cape to cape; upon his right arm rests
Northern Pelorum, on his left flung south
Pachynum, and on high above his feet,
Hopelessly captive, Lilybæum stands.
But o'er his head stupendous Etna rears
Her many-shouldered masses, through whose veins
Roars echoing his convulsive breath, and tears
Her struggling entrails; ever and anon,
To shift his weary flanks in effort vain,
He heaves his mighty chest; then tremors vast
From his portentous striving shake the land;
Then doth he writhe and bellow, and for spite
Spumeth forth flames and molten rocks in flood,
That blister all the mountain slopes with heat,
And waste the fruitful valleys leagues around.
Such rage, though calcined by the bolts of Zeus,
The Titan still hath strength to vomit forth
In hot insatiate floods of fiery surge.

  So told he, but they listened half-aroused,
As men whom dull narcotics have benumbed
In ear and eye, or who, with senses strained
Towards far-off scenes, will hearken unto words
Half-caught, and gaze on sights they do not heed.
So they in stupor of abasement heard

Unstirred, and lay in listless silence round,
Till slumber overgrew their lethargy.
For famine, cold, and fever, and all ills
That e'er beset so large a company
Voyaging over land and sea, in times
When half the earth was barren, void of men
And stores of food, and all her scarce-tried ways
Were slow and hard and long, now threatened
    them ;
And close upon them lay the dreaded straits,
Where Scylla leagued with grim Charybdis lurked
For hapless seamen ; but to linger then
Were but to die of hunger ; faint at heart,
They clomb aboard once more; with quaking souls
They watched the crags that seemed to close on
    them,
Like monstrous things of prey that crouched and
    crawled
In act to spring ; shrill o'er the howling blast
They heard the hovering Harpies laugh and call
From mast and cord ; their powerless oars rolled
    loose
Among the prostrate rowers ; jostling seas,
At war with storm and current, hurled them round

Hither and thither towards the imminent death
Looming from reef and cavern, that gave back
Their din redoubled unto wind and wave.
The staring helmsmen, grey with terror, clung
To rudders triple manned, and riven sails
Streamed back from shivering masts that writhed
        and groaned,
As though they lived; when on a sudden, lo!
The last crag lay behind them, and they rode
Astonied, safe on the Tyrrhenian Sea.

  Then women wept for joy and for relief,
And many an outworn man wept with them; soon
From littered decks a hopeful clamour rose,
And sails were trimmed anew, and oars ran out,
E'en songs were sung, and glad of heart they set
Their course for Cyrnus: many an hour they toiled
Aiding the fitful breeze, as men who nerve
Their limbs to one supernal effort strained,
Believing it the last; yet not for them
Had envious Fortune spent her stores of ill;
Outburst at nightfall from the deep-banked North
A furious gale that swept them towards the coast
Of western Italy, hard by a spot,
Lucanian Helea, a town new built,

Unknown to them whom tempest drave so near,
By offshoot settlers from Alalia ;
Above the mouth of Hales, in that bay
Which spreads between the Enipean Cape
And those sad headlands in the aftertime
By goodly Maro fabled to be named
Of shipwrecked Palinurus ; here might they
Welcome and kin have found, perchance an end
To all their weary travel ; but they failed
To compass land ; for once again the wind,
Veering at sundown, blew them from the coast ;
And ere the morning dawned they saw the cliffs
Of dark Sardinia, by men's fancy named
Ichnusa then, as like in form the print
Of some vast Titan's foot ; no profit there
To anchor, for to rest had been to die ;
Food had they none, and one more wintry night
Of starving bivouac had wrought their doom.
So, wellnigh shorn of hope, they kept the sea ;
The wind had fallen light, and helped them now ;
And silent, yielded to the hand of fate,
They let the fleet creep northward through the day.

Most wretched were they ; on each deck a crowd

Of gaunt and sickly starvelings sat, who strained
Their gaze towards the blank North; listless they
    crouched
With hair unkempt, and faces scarred and frayed,
And blistered arms they scarce knew how to raise,
And hands that bled ere well they clasped an oar,
And garments stained and faded, rotting, torn,
With sun, and rain, and sea-foam, and rough toil.
Ere sundown all the breeze had died away,
And e'en a treacherous current sliding through
Taphros, the strait that sunders the two Isles,
Began to cheat them towards the south again.
Then fell it for the first time that their crews,
Faint, sullen, self-abandoned, as a hare
Sits hopeless in the front of the close pack,
Failed at the oars, and dropped their bleeding
    hands
In speechless mutiny; not unforeseen
That moment of supreme despondency,
Nor unprepared their leaders; at a sign,
High on the prow of a great ship which sailed
Midmost, well seen of all the fleet, stood forth
Their Minstrel; on his gilded harp, his robe,
His flowing hair, and purple fillet, streamed

The rays of the low sun; his fiery hand
Swept through the chords, and with indignant mien,
And stern rebuke to every falterer
Throughout the lagging fleet, he called and sang.

    Row on, row on, 'tis Freedom's wing
        That many a day hath fanned our sails,
    Her tones that made the cordage ring,
        Her breath that swelled the eastern gales :
    Brave Asian gales, that oft ere now
    Have swept the fleet from stern to prow.

    Row on, row on, the wind hath ceased,
        As ever towards the eventide,
    No fleece-clouds gather in the east,
        In molten gold the west is dyed ;
    'Tis time yon listening shores should hear
    Our great oars creak from tier to tier.

    Row on, row on, ye have not borne
        And dared so long to falter thus ;
    It were enough to move the scorn
        E'en of the gods who favour us :
    When knew ye not Fate's prime decree
    That men must suffer to be free !

Oh think, my children, how ye toiled
    When that fierce Mede had hemmed us round,
And how the fretting tyrant, foiled
    E'en on his eve of triumph, found,
To take the shattered gateway's place,
Our new towers laughing in his face.

Remember with what scorn ye paid
    Those Chian caitiffs who denied
That gift of barren rock we prayed,
    Dreading to see us at their side,
E'en on Ænussæ's niggard shore,
Their betters both in peace and war.

And how we drave our prows once more
    Indignant o'er the dancing foam,
And purged with the invader's gore
    Each threshold of our ravished home;
Then left, for Medes to slay or bind,
Our dross of recreant souls behind.

Oh that my voice and harp had power,
    However faintly, to recall

How in that last tumultuous hour
   Ye spurned the proffered ease of thrall ;
When, fired by your enkindling rage,
I heaved and flung our massy gage.

And ere its fateful iron sank
   Into the keeping of the sea,
Ye all acclaimed from rank to rank
   The vow that bound us to be free,
And seek new homes beyond the main
Till our lost pledge should rise again.

Oh stamped in true heroic mould,
   Since that proud morning when we sailed,
Thirst, famine, fever, heat, and cold,
   Ye have borne all and never failed :
No peril of the land or sea
Hath cost us one heart's constancy !

Row on, row on, broad Etna's crest
   Hath sunk beneath the southern sky ;
Far off, unseen, in dewy rest
   Œnotria's low-couched valleys lie ;

A score or two of patient hours
And we shall sight Alalia's towers.

Then, courage, children, wheresoe'er
   Great deeds are henceforth loved and sung,
Phocæa's warrior-sons shall share
   The tribute of the poet's tongue ;
And our great vow to Freedom paid
Shall live till Freedom's self shall fade !

Long ere he ceased, his force divine had spread
Like flame among the embers of their souls ;
From ship to ship the bright contagion flew ;
Once more lean hands that late so listless hung
Clutched firm the creaking oars ; upon lean arms,
Late so relaxed, the knotted muscles strove ;
" Row on, row on," their newborn chorus rang,
" Row on, row on," the very children sang ;
And where an hour agone hung brooding gloom
Now all was blithe with work and merriment.
  Behind Sardinia's hills the sun sank down,
And left the ruddy-skirted heavens to hail
The full-faced moon ; slow climbed her welcome orb
The limpid east ; like balm her mildness fell

On the soothed exiles; through night's placid hours
Floated light harp-notes, and above these rose
Snatches of gladsome and familiar songs,
To cheer the fainting heart or wavering hand.
When on a sudden while the dawn's white robes
Silvered the fringes of the eastern verge
One from the mast-head of the foremost ship
Shouted "Alalia!" Upon deck and prow,
Bulwark, and stern, upshot a thousand forms,
And through a forest of wild waving arms
Rang but one cry of joy, "Alalia!"
For in the north a flickering flame leapt up,
And died and leapt again; the light it was
Of half-spent watch-fires blazing over sea,
Such as men kindle when they dread surprise
Of foemen under cover of the night,
And fain would have their warders scan the main.
With new-knit force the rowers swung; the day
Grew clear, and clearer grew the sighted town;
Soon were they ware of galleys ploughing swift
The intervening ocean space, intent
To prove them friend or foe; in one short hour
Met the two fleets with loud acclaim; their tale
Was short to tell; and ere the sun rode high

Beached in their kinsmen's haven lay their ships,
And their great voyage to Freedom vowed was o'er.

   Roll on, unresting Mother, it may be
That thou art not less mortal than thy sons,
And one day shalt float purposeless and dead
E'en as the very dead who float with thee!
It may be that we magnify thee now,
In deeming thee worth note among the worlds,
That all our reverence, love, and awe of thee
Are but reflections of a strange conceit
Wherewith we drape ourselves, and but provoke
A passing gibe among contemptuous spheres.
Nathless, roll on, the Little One of Space,
Of us the Mighty Mother! Bring us forth,
Caress, oppress, nurture, and torture us!
Be thy broad breast our cradle, home, and grave,
The battlefield whereon we war for life,
That life thou givest and we cannot keep,
But strive with thee to sweeten, with ourselves
To broaden and uplift; our conflict o'er,
Receive us and forget us! We will lie
Contented, if at whiles along thy years
Some deed, whereto each one of us hath lent

His little share of impulse, some emprise
Oblivion cannot master, shall be done,
Born of us all, though by a handful done,
That shall illume thy history, and redeem
Thy littleness among the mightier orbs,
The magnates of the universe; meanwhile,
Albeit our very bones have suffered change
Back into thee, we will sleep on, and wait
A call in the far-cycling deeps of Time.

SPRING.

THE sun is up, and the lark too;
   In morning dress of April dew
   Our lawns are grey;
Light western airs, like handmaids, bring
A tender message from the Spring,
   They seem to say,
" Why liest thou so late, my beloved?

" I am the Spring who call for thee ;
Wilt thou not wake to welcome me?
   I miss the grace
Wherewith thy goodly presence crowned
The beauties I have showered around
   This favoured place ;
Come forth, come forth, 'tis late, my beloved ! "

Spring.

Ah, hapless Spring, he may not come,
His eyes are locked, his voice is dumb,
    His heart is cold;
He doth not hear thy vestals keep
Their vigil o'er his dreamless sleep
    Beneath the mould;
He will not wake again, thy beloved.

NAAMAN THE SYRIAN.

PREFATORY NOTE TO "NAAMAN THE SYRIAN."

THIS poem needs a word of preface. It is an attempt to domesticate the Sapphic metre. Those who are conversant with that scheme know that the middle foot of each of its three lines is a dactyl, and that, by shifting the cæsura, two main types of rhythm are obtained. Of these, one throws an accent upon the first syllable of the dactyl, and the following lines are specimens of it in Greek, Latin, and English :

> Φαίνεταί μοι κῆνος ἴσος θεοῖσιν.
> Laurea donandus Apollinari.
> Green aloe groups springing about the sandheaps.

The other type throws the accent upon the second syllable of the dactyl. Of this the following are specimens :

Καὶ γὰρ αἰ φεύγει ταχέως διώξει.
Impios parrae recinentis omen.
Gathered in Edom over all her valleys.

The change from one to the other of these types and their variants diversifies pleasantly the cadence of the stanza. The poetess who gave her name to the metre avails herself largely of this liberty, but Horace adheres almost unfailingly to the second, and, to my ear, by no means the finer form. I have tried to follow Sappho rather than Horace, and have used both types indiscriminately.

For the rules of classical quantity, which are inapplicable to English, accent and correctness of ear and judgment are the only substitutes in the determination of the value of syllables.

NAAMAN THE SYRIAN.

LONE in his summer palace of Damascus,
    Lone with his pain sat Naaman, in anguish
Chief, as in fame, most hideously mingled,
    Leper and hero

Lone with his pain; his such a pain as kneadeth
All to its self, gathering force from all things,
Wealth, honour, all the heritage of heroes,
    Wasting as flame wastes.

Round the hall, divinely full-eyed, colossal,
Unbenign, calm, insuperably smiling,
Changeless, insensate, as the senseless sun beams
    Down on a lost land,

Ranged the carven Gods; and beyond the portals
Bloomed a green court where hooded grasses
    trembled

Round water-jets, and easy cypress alleys
    Swung in the sunlight.

There sat he, with beauty and peace and splendour
Mocked ; a waste feast of unenjoyed enjoyments
Spread to his eyes, within his heart a sense of
    Barren achievement

Burning with hate of happiness and beauty
Given to mean men ; his not the pride that throneth
Life upon torture overcome, and taketh
    Woe for an empire.

Then arising sudden unbidden harp-notes
Gentle, and full, and timorous, athwart the
Plashing of jets and rustle of the grass plumes,
    Quelling them all, came ;

Chaunt of heart-strokes, yearning, akin to sorrow,
Love-tremors spent, sighing "we suffer with thee ;"
Wastrels of prayer, climbing in vain the passive
    Knees of the dumb Gods.

These, as they grew round him, a voice o'ergrowing
Rose, and they fell, yielding it place, as twilight
Yields, or low winds, ushering in the morning,
    Faint in the sun's light.

Came the words, " May I pity thee, my master,
I that am lone too in a land of strangers ?
Would that these Gods could pity thee, and hear
    me !
    Then would thy healing

"Come, as Spring comes mantling in wasted valleys ;
Come, as warm song kindling with utterances
Dead caverns ; or love to a slave's heart, making
    Joy of its anguish.

" Oh, ye dumb Gods, why are ye not as my God
Dwelling in Zion, or as his priests your priests ?
Have ye no servants like the Lord Elisha
    Mighty to heal men ?"

He, sitting with hands rigid and lips parted,
Heard ; and, his heart aching for hope unhoped for,
Slowly, with pain, passed to the storied portals ;
    There by the fountain

Knelt a young slave damsel, a maid of Judah,
Fair as song's self and tremulous as echo :
" Tell me, this priest, what is he, girl, who keepeth
    Health for the wretched ?"

So for her gracious pity spake he graceless,
Graceless and blind ; she not the less rejoicing,
Plunged with quick tongue through every village
    wonder
    Told of Elisha.

Told him how Jordan's smitten flood receded ;
Swam the lost axe-head ; how a bitter fountain
Changed at his touch ; how, without rain or
    tempest,
    Floods in the drought-time

Gathered in Edom over all her valleys,
When the three kings and triple hosts lay helpless
Gazing at death ; how to the dead in Shunem
    Life at his order

Once returned. He, slowly, without a blessing,
Left her ; and said, " Surely the man who keepeth

Life for dead peasants hath a cure for princes."
So on the morrow

Past the long streets dark with the shade of banners,
Jubilant crowds shouting, "The Gods amend thee!"
Veiled women, silent upon house-tops, raising
Hands for a blessing,

Rode his array; and at its head the maiden,
Smiling unveiled upon the hills before her,
Hermon, and Bashan, and the slopes of Argob
Hiding the Jordan.

Bright the snow shone wreathing the heads of
Hermon,
Bright the oak crests spreading on woody Bashan,
Bright the grass downs clothing the slopes of Argob,
Brighter her young face

Flooded with hope; "Unto the hills," she murmured,
Gazing, her fingers in her harp-strings straying,
"Lift I mine eyes, unto the hills, the hills whence
Cometh my helper!"

Through the days thus, musing at whiles, or
        breaking
Into fresh ecstasies of song, whereunder
Softest undertones of the ready harp-strings
        Rose, as the rustle

Rises in quick aspen or airy willow,
When a sudden capricious ardour seizeth
Throstle and finch, and easy summer winds breathe
        Low for an answer,

Rode the sweet maid; while far away behind her,
Crouching in silence over rein and pommel,
Stretched the long lines of Syrians; the lithe-limbed
        Clambering horses

Clawed the steep downs, with quivering feet
        mastered
Stony ways worn through terebinth and oak groves,
Crept with close flanks round giddy ledges, slid down
        Dry watercourses,

Wound among unlovely ravines and hillsides
Blistered and grey; thus to the fords of Jordan

Slowly they came, and to the vale of Shechem,
    Fairest of all vales,

Mounted at morn; the barren lengths of Ebal
Flamed; a sweet haze of olive-tufted cornlands
Rose over Zalmon and the woody skirts of
    Holy Gerizim.

They along Shechem, under all the lavish
Wealth of showered shade, and melodies of song-
    birds
Hidden in wayside oliveyard and vineyard,
    Rode; and at noon saw

Ephraim's pearl, Samaria the matchless,
Lapped in rich hills, lie like a queen reclining,
Languorous, o'erlooking the western waters
    Far over Sharon.

Mute the long line, still at its head the maiden,
Street by street passed threading the town of Omri,
Till with sudden ringing of mail and harness,
    Stamping of horse-hoofs,

All the clash and clatter of armed men halting,
Round a rough space nigh to the western portal,
Ended their long march at the lowly roof where
    Tarried Elisha.

Turned to her master then the eager maiden,
But as she turned, bending across the threshold
Came one who said: " I, even I, Gehazi,
    Wait on Elisha.

" Thus to thy lord, damsel, my lord, Elisha,
Speaketh ; ' Depart, wash seven times in Jordan,
And be thou clean.' " Then, without further speech, he
    Turned him and left them.

Pale the while, stern, crushing the crowd of tortures
Long repressed, hearkened Naaman ; in silence
Stood the troop, and with timid eyes the maid sat
    Watching her master.

Him was pride, affronted and helpless, tearing
Worse than his pain ; " Surely, I thought," he
    murmured,

Naaman the Syrian. 89

"He will come forth, call on a God, and heal me!"
    Then in his anger,

" Are not," he cried, "O prophet, in thy judgment
Abana and Pharpar, rivers of Damascus,
Better than all these waters of thy country?
    May I not wash there?"

So the poor headstrong Syrian, and left him;
Nursing his pride and his disease together;
Nursing two hideous leprosies, twin curses,
    Blindly resentful.

Yet for some brief space at the lowly dwelling
Waited he lest the prophet should recall him,
Waited, as on his pleasure in Damascus,
    Waited her highest.

Smote on his steed with cruel heel, and started
Sweating with wrath and agony; behind him
Came the long line of followers, who feared him,
    Moodily riding.

Heedless of grouped villagers gravely gazing,
Heedless of terraced oliveyards and orchards,
Vines, and of fair corn patches rare on uplands
    White for the harvest,

Heedless of Judah's overmastering mountains,
Glistering peaks and myriad-hued recesses,
Heedless of sweet thorn thicket, flowery plains, and
    Palms by the well-side,

Green aloe-groups springing about the sandheaps,
Stream-riven breadths of tamarisk and willow,
Red ravines rich with oleanders, hillsides
    Stately with oak groves,

Heedless of all, and for the nightfall eager,
Feeding his spleen rode Naaman; till evening
Fell, and o'ertook him at the falls of Jordan,
    Forcing a halt there.

Bright at his tent's foot over ledge and boulder
Sparkled quick shallows; and beyond, the sunset
Lay, as health lies glowing about a child's cheek,
    Flushing a deep pool.

He within sat struggling the while the sun sank
Low, and left one half of the stream in darkness,
Flooding a green slope on the eastern margin;
    Then in the stillness

Close by his tent the little maid of Judah,
Eager, in fear, yet timorously daring,
Came with her harp, and hidden where a thornbrake
    Closed on the water,

Knelt; and with half voice, like the half lights
    round her,
Sang to her lord, invisible as her song's self,
Save that her white arms glimmered, and her fingers
    Flashed on the harp-strings.

" Abana and Pharpar, rivers of Damascus,
Fairer, ah me! how pitilessly fairer,
Than is this Jordan that I love! yet would I
    Well it were fairest,

" Only for this hour; that my master mastered
Haply might plunge; ah, why not plunge, my
    master?

See the sad sun sinketh away reluctant,
    Yet with his last rays

" Flusheth this flood and emerald marge yonder ;
Plunge, ere he pale, like a spurned God with-
    drawing ;
Plunge, the good gift may, while a lost hour
    passeth,
    Pass as a lost hour !"

Then in his dark tent, as the summer lightening
Rouses at nightfall all the sullen east, so
Did an insurmountable impulse stir in
    Him as he heard her.

Started he forth, rending away the gold pins
From the soft night-robe that he wore, and rushing
Past the low beds of pebbles by the shallows
    Plunged in the red pool.

And as he plunged, the dying glow to westward
Marred the moon's beams most hideously o'er his
Ulcerous limbs and body foully wasted ;
    But as he clomb forth

Up the green slope of flowered turf before him,
Fell the two lights harmoniously round him,
E'en as they fell round Adam once, the flawless,
  Walking in Eden.

Him awhile mute immeasurable wonder
Held; then his glee beat in him like a boy's glee,
So that he leapt, shouted, and, with arms waving,
  Stamped on the bright ground.

Plunged, replunged, profusely docile and ardent,
Breasting the muddled water, flinging backward,
Like a war-steed flinging his crest, the regal
  Plaits of his black hair.

Then a fresh Sidonian robe they brought him,
Shouting, and praising for a God the Jordan,
Shouting, and praising for a God Elisha,
  Drunk with the wonder.

But when he reached that thicket at his tent's door,
'Neath the thorn still the little maid of Judah
Stood, her white form gleaming against the trunks, as
  Gleameth a moonbeam.

Beautiful, helpless, broken as some stream breaks
Breaking itself, so with her soul's excess she
Quaking, and with unmanageable gladness,
    Fronted her master;

Longing for song, but all her voice dropped from her
Palsied in sobs; and quivering and nerveless,
As a spent wave strives at the beach, her fingers
    Strove in the harp-strings.

He in his joy, mindful of her sweet pleading,
Passed to his tent door, bade his people bring her;
Blessed her, and said, "Thou 'twas who freed me,
    damsel,
    Shall I not free thee?

"Nay, may thy God strike me anew, aye, blast me
Thousandfold more, if by this hour to-morrow,
Laden with treasures fit for queens, thou art not
    Telling this wonder

"Unto thy kindred!" Then he stooped and kissed
    her;
Bade her farewell, passing within the tent door;
Fell its folds; and the flooded eyes that loved him
    Lost him for ever.

SUMMER.

I PARDON not the song-thrush singing
    By thy lone bed,
Nor truant seagull idly winging
    Far o'er thine head ;
All blithe things fret me, wood-doves calling,
The whispering pine-tree, streamlet brawling,
Days rising fair or fairer falling,
    Now thou art dead !

Yet is the heart-tilth still as tender
    Where thy love grew,
And, as it rendered once, could render
    Greetings anew
To bridegroom snipe in mid air drumming,
Lambs bleating, honey-gleaners humming,
May's smiles and tears o'er sweet June's coming,
    Couldst thou come too.

ERIPHANIS.
AN IDYLL.

ERIPHANIS, one of the cyclic poetesses, was a native of Argos. She was of high birth and great beauty, but she accustomed herself to life in the woods, in order that she might marry the hunter Menalcas. (Athenæus xiv. 206.)

ERIPHANIS.

THESE are the fairest woods of Argolis,
    And dwelling with Menalcas in their midst,
Brave, beautiful Menalcas, my bold hunter,
I am the happiest of the Argolids.
    Brave, beautiful Menalcas, my bold hunter!
He came and wooed me long ago in Argos
With woodland gifts, and stories of the woods,
And of their beauty and the life in them.
And I began to love him from the first;
And ofttimes from the first would sigh and say,
Communing cautiously with mine own soul,
Lest he should see and press his vantage on me,
"Thy woods can scarce be fairer than thyself,
And life with thee were lovely anywhere."
Yet—for I dreaded then to give my heart
Its freedom, and to cut the gilded chains
That bound me to my mean luxurious days
Among the rich in rich and idle Argos,

And for I dreaded too the gibing tongues
Of men and women, and their false contempt
And falser pity for brave love—whene'er
His spirit seemed to question mine, I lied
By an ignoble silence, or else laughed
A laugh that did the office of a lie.

   But, when I paltered thus, he would step back
Among the pillars of the gleaming hall,
The blushes of rebuked nobility
Shrouding his face; while I, coward and fool,
Well knowing that I wronged my heart and him,
Would o'er self-censure draw the rags of pride,
And cross to some gay group of Argolids
To drown in jest the sense of mine own shame.

   Noble Menalcas! I have never dared
To learn what then thy tortured soul endured.
For one, scarce out of earshot of the man,
With that pert folly they call wit in towns,
Would thus begin: "What, my Eriphanis,
Not ridded of thy Satyr yet? This grows
Of having fed him when he came astray!
He'll follow thee for ever now." And so
Another would sigh drawling, "Ah, poor beast!
Send word to Bacchus or to Pan to fetch him;

Eriphanis.

Some Dryad, doubtless, stays beneath her oak,
Pouting and pining for her comely mate;
For the poor thing is comely after all."
    My beautiful Menalcas, my bold hunter!
Comely! Ah, let those mockers tell me who
Of all the youths, whom walking in white Argos
Their sidelong eyes beset, is comelier!
Who hath a goodlier carriage, or whose limbs
Are white as thine beneath thy hunter's dress?
Or who could spring like thee to bend thy bow,
Mine Archer-God, my Phœbus of the woods,
—Thy bow that would not answer to their fingers—
While all thy clustering hair breaks out behind
Its bondage, and thy shapely limbs are poised,
In energy and grace alike divine!
    Brave beautiful Menalcas, my bold hunter!
Nor only for thy beauty and thy hunting
Like to the Archer-God who loveth thee.
For thou like him canst lay aside thy bow,
And shape thy fingers to another string.
Oft have I watched thee when the close of day
Found thee contented with thy counted spoils,
Propt on the gnarled root of some ancient tree
Or sauntering at ease from glade to glade,

With voice and lyre, which, after thy wild hunt,
Filled the soothed forest, as the zephyr fills
The places where the cleaving storm hath raged,
Draw back the scared wood-creatures up the lawns.
Panting, with outstretched neck and timorous eyes,
And limbs that seemed to totter, would they come,
Their sides still wet with anguish and the chase,
While the long columns of their weary breath
Drave in the evening air; for a brief space,
With many a doubtful halt, and sudden turn
Of ear and eye, they would step trembling on;
Till calmed at length by music, that had grown
Well-known and welcome as the sunset hour,
First one and then another would bend down,
Till the last lines of western light would fall
On silent browsing groups, and bedded groves
Of antlers tossing o'er the peopled fern.

Oh, my Menalcas, my well-chosen husband!
We Argolids in Argos knew no life,
And deemed none worth the living, save our own.
Not to partake the fashion of our lot
We held was to be wretched, strange, and rude.
And all that vast and beauteous expanse
Of multitudinous and happy fates,

Lying beyond the poor and narrow bound
That measured our disdainful ignorance,
We merged in a contemptible contempt.
Oh, pride accursed in which I stooped to take
My portion with the others! Littleness,
Wherein with them I cooped my nature down!
Oh, mean and coward fear, wherewith I strove
Like them to fetter all in me that yearned
To hazard one free act, to mount and set
The sails of being to the wind, and turning
A glad prow to the bounding seas of Fate,
Never look back on the cramped roadstead more!
For, long before I ceased to spurn thee, came
The knowledge that I loved thee, and my scorn
Fell back upon myself in burning showers.
And every gibe of their vain girlish lips,
Shaped in mean concert to my seeming humour,
And every coward laugh I laughed with them,
Rose like a blister on my heart, and heated
My fever of self-hatred higher. So,
The months went by, and heavier grew the mask,
And, failure after failure, heavier
The effort to uplift it; though one word
Had been enough. Had I but risen, and said,

"Cease, for I love him," I had turned at once
To flattery every taunting lip, and waked
A harmony of chatter in thy praise.

   At length one autumn eve I sat alone
Before the hearth-fire in my father's hall.
The last low breadth of ruddy sunlight lay
Glowing among the columns, and above,
High in the fretted ceiling, on the coils
Of smoke that gathering clomb, and slowly crept
Out through the dusky timbers of the roof,
Flickered and flushed the mimicry of flame.
I had been musing on my home and life,
And how I theretofore had hoped to live;
Thinking what pain it was to crush out love
For love of other things; and then, what pain
To cast all other things away for love.
And whether hearts where love hath been, and gone,
Can take the glow of pleasure as of old,
Or must for evermore be lit by love,
Or lie for ever dark. "And if," thought I,
"To keep alive the treasured joys of youth,
The heart itself that treasures them must die,
What good comes of the thrift? What good to
      move

Cold and uncaring through the splendid crowds,
Walking through pleasures as a blind man walks
Through beauty with his blank and listless eyes?
Who dreams of beauty who dreams not of love?
And what—save that we hope for love at last—
Were splendour, and the never-ending round
On which wealth carries us by night and day,
But weary brightness and laborious pomp?
Is Argos then the world, or Argive life
The summit and the archetype of all?
Is all else cheerless, graceless, fashionless?
Hath the broad range of human happiness
Shrunk round one little company? Are none,
Who are not of us, what we deem ourselves?
Can I not go hence and be still myself?
Will my poor beauty perish in the woods,
For lack of its old Argive flatterers?
Or shall I cease to love and cherish it?
Will my light gifts of wit and poesy
Dwindle like plants in an unsheltered air?
Or will they flourish in a freer scene,
Tended by leisure and watched o'er by love?
In Argos men and women seek alike
To draw themselves to pattern, lest they lose

The impress of a fashion; and for this
They shear and pare their very gifts away,
Each lowering each in efforts to be like.
Of all this in the woods I may be free;
And what lies now unhonoured and unused,
May grow besides a pleasure and a power.
Perchance I may give luxury for life,
As heretofore my life for luxury;
Perchance I go to knead the love of arts,
That town-bred folk have well-nigh ceased to love,
Into the simpler and unsated lives
Of hunters, shepherds, and rough husbandmen.
So that my nature now clipped down and shorn
To the trim hedgerow of society,
May branch abroad, afresh in a fair field,
To mine own honour and the general good.
Menalcas hath said much of such a life,
And how he scarce can compass it alone,
Without a helpmate. To it I will go."

So, half in speech, and half in thought alone,
Little by little, did my soul come forth,
And open out into its full resolve;
As in the bursting bud, fold flings back fold,
And petal upon petal spreads and grows

About the rim of the fast broadening flower.
And then I rose and paced about the hall;
And stretched mine arms aloft, and laughed, and
    sighed,
And felt as those who have been long perplexed,
Or long in dread, but are no longer so.
And in a little while I went without,
And took my way under some cypresses
That flanked a terrace in the garden, set
With flowery urns and statues of the Gods,
All gleaming in the moonlight; there I sought
A seat beneath the cypresses, and so,
Still musing, sat me down in the deep shade.
And while I sat unseen, a spasm of pain
Beat through me; for I heard from the dark end
Of the long terrace, in deep half-hushed tones,
The voice of my Menalcas; he had come,
As now I know he oft had come before,
Hopeless, to haunt my home in his unrest.
Still was the night, and I on fire to hear;
But—for he spake so low, and to himself—
I crept along the turf, close by the trees,
Panting with eagerness and stealthy fear.
And when I came where I could listen well,

I stopped, with one hand grasping at the boughs,
The other clutched over my plunging heart.
And thus I heard him in his agony,
Repeating some wild fragment of a verse,
That he had made in dalliance with his woe,
Chiding himself:

"Wilt thou not close thine eyes?
This is too lovely for thy peace; it wears
A charm both delicate and perilous;
Thou art but weakly yet; nay, close thine eyes;
Linger no more!

"Still gazing? Through thy fascinated sight
Stealeth the beauty that undoth thee. Come;
'Tis thus dead sorrows do inhale new life,
And thine reviveth even now. Return;
Linger no more!

"Alas, alas! Thy look is changing fast,
Thine eyes are setting to a wasted calm,
Thy lip hath fallen trembling, and thy limbs
Hang listlessly; and this is beauty's work!
Linger no more!

"The ills that time inflicts and will not heal,
Helpless and hopeless are to those alone
Who chain themselves as slaves thereto; such sow
Their puny longings, and they reap despair.
Linger no more!"

    He paused, or seemed to pause and move away;
And I, in a quick ecstasy of fear,
Lest he should go for ever, and undo
The peace that he had won for him and me,
Sprang forth into the moonlight, crying out,
"Nay, stay, stay, for I love thee, and am changed!"
He for a space stood still and dumb; and then,
With one long staggering bound o'er the low wall,
Came crashing through the terraced flowers, and
    stood
Fronting me, with his keen o'er-shaded eyes
And yearning face pressed forward near to mine.
One wistful look up to the heavens he turned,
As though he would ask aid of the weak moon
To shed a clearer light, and let him solve
His wonder from my fixed and faded eyes.
And even while he looked, I felt my heart
Pause, and about me a swift darkness grew.

I knew his arms were round me as I fell,
And heard a cry; and in a while I found
My father bending o'er me, as I lay
Propt on a long bench in the hall; and saw
Menalcas with him; and I knew that all was well.

And all was well, and is, and would be more,
Could it but be for ever; and could all
That I have learned and gained from a wise love
Be taught broad-cast among my friends of old.
For dearer far than e'er white Argos was,
Its ordered streets, and marble-fronted fanes,
Pillars and porticoes, are these sweet lands;
These pastoral slopes blinking beneath the sun,
Streaked with white wavy lines of winding flocks,
And fretted o'er with ruddy groups of kine;
And these rich forest belts that gird us round,
And, stretching far below us, hem the throne
Of the deep heavenly mountains far aloft,
Gleaming with peak, and crag, and cone, and spire,
And dark with mystery of gorge, and cave,
And cataract shrouded in the dim ravine.
And free, and full of grace and joy, my life
Among these simple people of the woods;

And worthier far the honour that they give
Than the false homage to my beauty paid
In the old days, for it is better won.
For something do they surely owe to me.
They owe to me the songs the shepherd sings
Along the windy tracks on the lone hills;
The forest legends that the woodcutter
Tells to his fellows at their midday meal;
And all the stories of the war for Troy,
And poems of the Gods, that old and young
Crowd from the household hearths on winter nights.
To hear the good-wife chaunt behind her loom.
To me they owe, for fierce were they and rude,
The love of beauty in all things, and all
That man is called to do; and of these, chief
The love of right because 'tis beautiful,
Of gentleness, and love, and household grace,
And order, and the peace of order born.
And of all these I reap the full reward,
And honour, in their general love and praise;
While they bless me who made them what they are,
And I my fate, in that I made them so;
For they are happy as their woods are fair.

AUTUMN.

OUR Beaulieu heath is still all dight
 In golden gorse and purple heather;
This walk was ever thy delight,
 And mine, when we could walk together.

Beneath my feet is fragrance spread,
 About mine ears the south wind sighing,
And surly cloudlets overhead
 Between me and the sun are flying.

These breadths of odorous flowery plain
 Smile like thy soul's remembered graces,
All sweet, all bright, without a stain,
 Save such as grief's first tear effaces.

But yon dark scud that sweeps across,
 Dims the gay tints, and chills the tender,
E'en as my cruel sense of loss
 Mars every boon thy past would render.

PER GLI OCCHI ALMENO NON V'È CLAUSURA.

PERUGIA holds a picture wrought by one
    Whose cunning hand, rich heart, and master eyes
Have drawn their mellow forces from the sun
    That ripens all things 'neath Etruscan skies;
A convent wall it is that tells his tale,
    Crag-built, breast-high; a grey Nun leans on it,
Gazing across a sweet home-teeming vale;
    And underneath for keynote has he writ,
      Per gl' Occh' almeno non v'è Claüsura.

We gaze with her, but know not whence we gaze—
    Some terraced perch perchance of Apennine—
For o'er his scene he spreads a studious haze
    That leaves mysterious what he found divine;
Nor may we raise the lappet of her veil
    To note if the clipped locks be gold or grey;

Nor ask whose spirit 'tis that thus breaks pale
    In one sad whisper to the summer day;
        Per gl' Occh' almeno non v'è Claüsura.

Her eyes are messengers that go and come
    To gild her soul with guesses; to make fair
The chambers of her mind, grown void and numb
    With painless penance and with prayerless prayer;
So may some manacled forgotten wretch
    Watch o'er his head chance swallow-shadows flit,
Blurring the shafts of light that faintly stretch
    Athwart the roof of his dark dungeon pit;
        Per gl' Occh' almeno non v'è Claüsura.

Life in those glancing shapes doth visit him,
    Life of the fields, the air, the sunny sky,
Warm eaves, the clay-built nest, the homestead trim,
    Byres, and the dovecote's burnished colony;
No longer rots he in his oubliette,
    But basks at large in sunshine, painless, free;
One glimpse; it flashed, and died, but leaves him yet
    A horde of happy dreams for progeny:
        Per gl' Occh' almeno non v'è Claüsura.

non v'è Clausura.

She straineth still her gaze across the plain
    That nought but a replete confusion seems
Of meads and tufted trees and sheeted grain,
    Now swathed in shade now basking in the beams:
So long, so motionless, she scanneth there
    All that divining love hath made her own,
That timid garden mice peep forth and stare,
    And lizards gambol near her on the stone ;
      Per gl' Occh' almeno non v'è Claüsura.

She counts the huddled hamlets one by one,
    Whose campanili top their clustering pines,
Marks every quivering stream that takes the sun,
    Orchards, and olive-gardens looped with vines ;
And spiny locust-trees along a road
    That threads the little bourg where she was born,
Then last, the whitewashed farm where once abode
    Hopes that her vows forbid her e'en to mourn ;
      Per gl' Occh' almeno non v'è Claüsura.

O patient eyes, what if your halting sweep
    Of eager search down from that mountain cage
Match but the fingers of the blind that creep,
    And falter, labouring o'er their fretted page !

And what, O fasting soul, if, sore in need,
   Thy faith to thine own feigning thou hast lent,
Like shipwrecked starvelings who are driven to feed
   On husk and herb that bear no nutriment!
     Per gl' Occh' almeno non v'è Claüsura.

Too like to us thou art, O soul fast hemmed,
   And ye too like to us, ye patient eyes,
We too are famine stricken, and condemned
   To cheat our cravings with sweet forgeries:
Pent up in life and time, with Death's high pale
   Between us and our lost ones, we are fain
To soothe our souls with dreams that less avail
   E'en than your musings o'er your Tuscan plain;
     Per gl' Occh' almeno non v'è Claüsura.

Like you we murmur, "Where and what are they?
   And are they happy? Do they love us yet?
Do their plumes ever take our earthward way?
   Or is our cell indeed an oubliette
Wherein we lie forgotten in our night,
   While they in effortless effulgence float

From marvel unto marvel, with the light
   Of their pure will for steed and chariot?"
     Per gl' Occh' almeno non v'è Claüsura.

We can but dream of them as once they were,
   Our visions are but symbols of their change;
White robes, steed, chariot, pinions, golden hair,
   Are but wild phantoms which our visual range
Compounds from mortal loveliness and power,
   Whereunder gleams the essence we adore;
We can but ransack earth their forms to dower
   With all we see, and puny is our store;
     Per gl' Occh' almeno non v'è Claüsura.

Who from its nest—who never knew a bird—
   Could dream of eagle's glance or swallow's flight,
Or how the nightingale with songs unheard
   Doth sanctify the silence of the night?
Who from a seed could hint the towering pine,
   Or guess the pendant fruitage of the palm,
The wine-stored clusters of the stooping vine,
   The blushing rose's lips and mystic balm?
     Per gl' Occh' almeno non v'è Claüsura.

Yet not, monastic Comrade, not in vain,
   We beat with baffled souls at prison bars,
Thou yearning for thy home in yonder plain,
   We tracking our lost treasure through the stars;
'Tis sweet to cheat ourselves a little while,
   And something gained it is for us and thee
An hour or two of longing to beguile
   In blindly murmuring "We see, we see!"
      Per gl' Occh' almeno non v'è Claüsura.

WINTER.

THE winter day is dying like the year,
    With warmth enough to call the bats around,
Behind our hill the young moon rises clear,
    And the swift night sweeps up without a sound.

With evening's parting crimson on her breast
    The full-lipped river glimmers in the meads;
The hungry snipe runs bleating on her quest,
    And cautious wild-fowl call among the reeds.

I stand alone amid the gathering gloom,
    While all the changes of the earth and sky
Pass over me, as over one with whom
    Proud Nature cares not to keep company.

But what is yonder dim and airy form
    That passed and now repasses overhead?
Why here, sweet seabird? No untimely storm
    Hath driven thee inland from thine ocean bed!

Winter.

The skies are calm, the silent waves asleep,
  And sleep thy snowy kindred miles away;
Why dost thou here a truant vigil keep,
  And wheel above these marshes, sweet one, say?

Above my head it sweeps and sweeps again,
  Turning a pure white bosom to the moon,
Anon it rises, spreads its wings amain,
  Flutes me one flying farewell, and is gone.

Farewell, farewell, bird, seraph, messenger,
  Whate'er thou art, Heaven speed thy winnowing
    plume;
Thy sight hath set my leaden soul astir,
  And I turn grateful homeward through the gloom.

THE
PROMETHEUS BOUND
OF
ÆSCHYLUS.

DRAMATIS PERSONÆ.

    Prometheus.
    Hephaistos.
    Kratos and Bia.
    Oceanus.
    Io.
    Hermes.
    Chorus of Oceanids.

Scene: *A mountain gorge in Scythia.*

PROMETHEUS BOUND.

Kratos.

SO unto this sequestered tract of earth,
 These lone untrodden ways of Scythia
Have we attained; Hephaistos, now 'tis thine
To take in hand our Father's charge to thee,
And to these high o'erhanging cliffs to rivet
This arch-transgressor, who hath dared to steal
For mortal use thy bright prerogative
And parent of all arts, engendering Fire.
For this 'tis meet unto the Gods he make
Full expiation, so that he may learn
To bear the sovereignty of Zeus, and curb
His bent perverse and passion for Mankind.

Hephaistos. Kratos and Bia, ye are free; your
 charge
From Zeus hath in fulfilment found its close.
For me, I shrink, albeit I must nerve
My heart thus far—so dire the peril were

To lay out of my sight our Sire's command—
My kinsman and a God besides to bind
To this inhospitable chasm.
[*To Prometheus.*]   O thou
High-purposed son of righteous Themis, now
Reluctant thee reluctant must I weld
To this lone peak ; here neither voice nor form
Of man shall reach thee ; here for blisters scorched
By flames of the fierce sun shalt thou exchange
The bloom of thy fair body ; to thine ease
The starry-kirtled night shall screen his blaze,
But to thine ease again shall he too scatter
The hoar-frosts of the morning ; ever thus
A weight of active and alternate pain
Shall wear thee, for Redeemer hast thou none.
Such fruit thou gatherest of thy love for Man ;
For to the wrath of Gods, thyself a God,
Too unsubmissive, thou didst lavish grace
On mortals ; therefore shalt thou keep thy post
Erect and sleepless, and with knees unbent
On these delightless crags ; full many a groan
And many a lamentation shalt thou waste :
For unassailable by prayer is Zeus,
And hard as all are who are new to power.

Krat. Go to; a truce to drivel and delay;
Why halt in hate of one whom all Gods hate,
One who, to boot, in making gifts to Man,
Hath played the traitor with thy privilege?
　Heph. Kinship and friendship are two solemn things.
　Krat. Agreed; but is it less to disobey
Thy Sire's behest? Which is the greater fear?
　Heph. Ruthless and reckless, this is naught to thee!
　Krat. I count it naught indeed to whine o'er him.
Waste not thy piety on idle uses!
　Heph. Oh, cursèd mastery of handicraft,
How I do loathe thee now!
　Krat.　　　　　　Why loathe it, friend?
'Tis not to blame for this.
　Heph.　　　　　Yet not the less
Would I some other had been dowered therewith.
　Krat. No fate is flawless, save supremacy;
And one alone is free, and he is Zeus.
　Heph. I know that, and I cannot answer thee.
　Krat. Why then, despatch; let not the Father turn
His glance upon thy hesitation; come!

Heph. Well, come; the chains lie handy, as thou seest.

Krat. Hammer them well about his hands, and deep
Into the solid rock-face drive the clamps.

Heph. 'Tis well-nigh done; I have not paltered with it.

Krat. Strike harder, brace all up, leave nothing slack;
His powers of shift are well-nigh infinite.

Heph. This arm at least is now securely braced.

Krat. Then buckle this as well; so let him learn,
This sage, how dull his wit when matched with Zeus.

Heph. No one, save him, can now complain of me.

Krat. Now drive this adamantine wedge's fang
Straight through his breast, and nail it sturdily.

Heph. Alas, Prometheus, how I pity thee!

Krat. Shrinking again, and moaning over foes
To Zeus? See that thou moan not for thyself!

Heph. You see a sight most horrible.

Krat.   I see
This fellow getting his deserts. But, come;
Strap and make fast the bands about his sides.

Heph. What I must do, I do! Order me not!

Krat. Aye, but I will, and hound thee on ! Now then,

Go down and firmly hoop those legs.

Heph. "Tis done,

And deftly done.

Krat. Now once more stoutly set

And both these galling anklets rivet firm.

Stern is the censor of thy work, remember.

Heph. So is thy tongue, attuned to fit thy form.

Krat. Play thou the soft heart, if it pleaseth thee ;

But gibe not at my qualities and temper.

Heph. Let us begone, his limbs are netted now.

Krat. Now run thy riot here, despoil the Gods

T'enrich thy friends, those creatures of a day !

I wonder, will they serve for thy relief?

Ill art thou called Prometheus ! To my mind

Thou needest a Prometheus for thyself

To show thee how to wriggle out of this !

[*Exeunt Hephaistos, Kratos, and Bia.*

Prom. Thou Empyrean Heaven, and you, ye Winds,

Fleet-pinioned, River Founts, and Waves who make

The countless dimples of the laughing seas,
And thou, great Mother Earth, and thou, O Sun,
Who from thy sphere maintainest orbèd watch
O'er all things, unto one and all I cry!
Look on me, me divine, at hands divine
What I endure; aye, look, and ponder how
Outworn by outrage I shall wrestle through
Time with its myriad years; such bonds of shame
The new-made Master of the Happy Gods
Hath forged for me. Alas, alas, alike
The present and the future, all is pain!
How shall I ever reach the end ordained!
Yet why ask this? Full clearly I foreknow
All that shall be; no unexpected pang
Shall ever seize me; naught becomes me, save
To bend to what awaits me, to make mine
Such ease as resignation brings, and bear
Fate and invincible Necessity.
Yet neither can I speak nor withhold speech
In this my misery; my durance comes
Of striving to endow Mankind; a reed
Stored with the fount of surreptitious fire
Hath wrought this persecution, yet shall prove
The source and master of all arts to Man.

That was my fault, and this my forfeit paid
In bonds beneath the canopy of heaven.
Ah me, ah me! [*After a pause.*]
What sound, what fragrance faint and silent, steals
About me? Mortal, or divine, or both?
What is it, and why comes it hitherward
To this outlandish peak? To gaze on me?
Who or whate'er ye be, ye see in me
A most ill-fated God, by hate of Zeus
Enchained, and universal enmity
Of all who come and go through Heaven's halls,
Hate bred of mine o'er-mastering love for Man.
Alas, alas! a quivering sound I hear
As of birds near me; all the air sings low
With lightsome sweep and rustle of many wings.
Whate'er approaches me, I tremble at it.

Chorus of Oceanids.

No need to tremble now,
For friendly comes my company
Unto this mountain-brow;
On emulous pinions did I fly,
Making fleet winds my convoy through the sky.
But scarcely could my pleading win

> Our Father's temper to my will,
> While beat on beat the stroke and din
> Of hammered iron woke the still
> Recesses of our caves afar,
> And striking, drove away grave-featured shame,
> So that unsandalled to this wingèd car
> I darted and I came.

Prom. Offspring of fruitful Tethys, children too
Of Father Ocean, whose unresting flood
Is rolling ever round the world, mark, mark,
How, staked and bound to the extremest crags
Of this ravine, I mount unenvied guard.

Chor. I mark, albeit affright
  A mist of tears with sudden hand
    Hath spread before my sight,
  Upon these rocks to see thee stand
Wracked in this shame of adamantine band;
  A pale and withering form thou art
  And shalt be, on Olympus now
  An upstart Master plays the part
  Of a new helmsman to the prow;
  And he, of will all uncontrolled,

Dispenses his new laws with wanton sway,
And all most mighty and revered of old,
   His arm doth sweep away.

Prom. Ah, would that under earth and far below
That infinite where Tartarus engulphs
The dead whom Hades gathers, I had been hurled
By wrath as savage into bonds as deep;
So that nor God nor mortal had exulted
O'er this my shame, nor I been left to make,
As thus I make to-day, ah! woe is me,
Sport for my foes and all the winds of heaven!

Chor. Which of the Gods is there,
  Save Zeus, from this thine evil plight,
  Hard-hearted, who would draw delight,
    And would not rather share
      These pains of thine?
But he, with rancour and with hate
Hath set his soul to subjugate
    Our heavenly line.
Nor will he ever cease until
He shall have wrought his utmost will,
    Or else meanwhile

Some venturous foeman shall arise
    Fated by force or guile
To hurl him from his stronghold in the skies.

Prom. Aye, of a surety yet, though here I lie
Outraged, in chains, at last a day shall dawn
When this new Master of the Happy Gods
Shall learn his need of me, me who alone
Can warn him from that fresh design, whereby
Of seat and sceptre he shall fall despoiled.
But this, nor chaunting of a honied tongue
Shall charm, nor menace cow me, to disclose,
Before he free me from these cruel bonds,
And pay me the requital of this shame.

Chor.   Bold, overbold thou art,
  E'en under torture yieldest naught;
  Nor thine unbridled tongue hast taught
    To play a prudent part;
    But I for thee
  Am thrilled through by a stabbing fear,
  Dreading what may befall thee here,
    And what may be
  The destined haven of thy woes;

Or how, or when, or where, the close;
   For Kronos' son
A heart impregnable doth bear,
   Not to be ever won
By words, or to be turned aside by prayer.

Prom. I know that he is hard, and that his will
Is his one code to him of right and wrong;
But nathless, pliable and mild of mood
Shall he become when this hath broken him.
And low his stubborn temper shall he lay
When, eager to me eager, he shall turn
For reconcilation and goodwill.

Chor. But tell me now thy tale from end to end,
Unless the telling pain thee overmuch;
Upon what imputation of misdeed
Hath Zeus reduced thee to this bitter shame?

Prom. Aye, pain is it, indeed, to tell the tale;
But silence too is pain; on all hands pain.
When first the Gods to strife betook themselves,
And general discord was aroused in Heaven,
Some wishing to cast Kronos from the throne
That Zeus might reign, others with adverse zeal
Alert, that Zeus might never rule the Gods,

Then I, to the best purpose counselling
The Titans, progeny of Earth and Heaven,
Failed; for in hard-set pride, of wiles and skill
Contemptuous, by force they thought to pluck
An easy triumph; but not once alone
Themis, my mother, Gaia she, one shape
Of many names, the issue had foretold,
How not to those in boldness or in force
Pre-eminent, but in craft, the mastery
Should finally incline; which when I urged,
They held my counsel but of little worth,
And me regarded not at all; then best
From all things left to choose it seemed to me,
Taking my mother with me, of free will
To range ourselves with those who stood for Zeus
'Twas through my counsels that the deep dark bays
Of Tartarus old Kronos have engulphed
With all his crew confederate; such a debt
The Monarch of the Gods incurred to me,
And this the measure of the ill reward
Wherewith he quits me! Power within itself
Doth ever bear this blight, mistrust of friends!
But now the head and front of mine offence,
For which you ask me, I proceed to tell.

No sooner sat he on his father's throne
Than straightway he began among the Gods
To portion office and prerogative;
But of unhappy mortals no account
He made, nay, had it in his mind
To work their extirpation, and to plant
Some new creation in their stead; 'gainst this
None stood save me; I braved him, and I saved
Man's race from sinking shattered into Hell.
For this am I laid low in agony
Dreadful to bear and piteous to behold.
And, for I gave Man pity, to receive it
Am worthless deemed, but pitilessly thus
Am ordered to the infamy of Zeus.

 Chor. Of iron-tempered soul and granite-wrought,
Prometheus, would he be, who failed to feel
Compassion for thy trouble; I never wished
To see, but seeing, I am sick at heart.

 Prom. Aye, 'tis a sight to make the pity of friends.

 Chor. But didst thou nothing more than thou hast told?

 Prom. I made men cease to brood upon their doom.

Chor. Where foundest thou the cure for that
    disease?
Prom. I set blind hopes to colonize their souls.
Chor. A mighty boon!
Prom.   And then I gave them fire.
Chor. What, have these poor Ephemerals flame-
    faced fire?
Prom. And many an art and craft shall learn of it.
Chor. And on such charges hath Zeus outraged
    thee
With pauseless tortures? Is there no term fixed?
    Prom. Nay, none but when he wills it.
    Chor.   But his will
What shall provoke? What hope? Dost thou not
    see
That thou hast erred? No pleasure 'tis to me
To tell thee thou hast erred, though pain to thee
To hear it; let us leave all this, and strive
If aught we may devise to set thee free.
    Prom. 'Tis a light thing for one who walketh free
Of evil to admonish and exhort
A friend in evil case. I knew all this.
Of mine own will I erred; I say it still.
To stay Man's ruin I have wrought my own.

Yet little thought had I in pains like these
To pine away on these uplifted crags,
This lone sequestered peak my heritage!
But spare your pity from these present ills.
Alight; hear what the future hath in store.
So may'st thou know the whole unto the end.
Ah, grace me, grace me thus; suffer thus far
With one who suffers; for, bethink thee well,
Woe is a wanderer, and as he goes
Hither and thither through all space and time,
Seeking new seats, he may alight on thee.

Chor. Prometheus, no reluctant ear
This pressure of thy prayer receives,
The fleet-winged car that bore me here
    My light foot leaves;

And from the air, whose bright pure space
Unto the birds a causeway lends,
Straightway upon this rock-strewn face
    Of earth descends.

I long to hear thee once again
Take up the story of thy pain.
    [*The Oceanids alight from their car.*

Enter OCEANUS *loq.*

Of my long travel hither have I reached
The goal at last, Prometheus; piloted
By this fleet bird, for whom my guiding will
Nor bit nor bridle needeth; be thou sure
I suffer with thy fortunes; kin alone
Would thus compel me, but apart from kin,
None liveth unto whom I deal my love
More largely than to thee; aye, true this is,
And no cheap chatter of a glozing tongue;
Essay me; say what I may do for thee,
And thou shalt straightway find there breatheth not
A friend more trusty than Oceanus.

 Prom. Ah me! what now? Hast thou too come to be
Spectator of my woes? How hast thou dared
To leave the flood that bears thy name, and caves
Unwrought, which Earth hath vaulted for thine home,
To seek these iron-teeming wilds? Com'st thou
To gaze and muse and grieve with me? Behold,
And wonder; look on me, the friend of Zeus,
The friend who helped to seat him on his throne,
How 'neath his hand I am bowed down in bane.

Ocean. I see, I see; and though I know thee wise
And subtle, I would fain admonish thee.
Review thyself, reform thy moods; the Gods
Have a new master now; if thou wilt hurl
These rough and sharply-whetted railings, Zeus
Throned on his heights remote may hear perchance,
And so to-day may come to seem to thee
Child's play alike in wrath and agony.
Oh, my unhappy friend, dismiss thy wrath,
And seek release. It may be that my words
Stale and unprofitable do sound to thee;
Yet not the less such as thou handlest now
Is e'er the wage of an o'erweening tongue.
But thou art not yet humbled, nor dost yield
To suffering; nay, thou stretchest out thine hands
For more; but not, with me for teacher, thou
Shalt kick against the pricks, seeing, as I see,
How hard and irresponsible is Zeus.
Now will I go, and such endeavour make,
As make I may, to win thee thy release.
Thou meanwhile hold thy peace, indulge no more
Thy turbulent ravings; what, dost thou not know,
Thou too so over-wise, that punishment

Lights ever on a levity of tongue?

 Prom. I do commend thy fortunes, thine, who art
Free of my condemnation, having shared
My venture to the uttermost. Let be!
Nay, meddle not with Him, it were in vain;
He is not made to yield; look to thyself;
I would not that this journey wrought thee harm.

 Ocean. I do avouch thy power, by word and deed,
To teach thy neighbour, rather than thyself.
Seek not to draw me back from my resolve;
I have no fear, no fear, I say, but Zeus
Shall grace me with the boon of thy reprieve.

 Prom. I thank thee, and shall never cease, aye,
  never,
To praise thee for this fulness of thy zeal;
But spare thy pains, they were in vain, whate'er
Thy readiness, and profitless to me.
Be still, content thee with thine own escape;
Enough that I should suffer! 'Twould not make
My solace to sow suffering broadcast; no!
Ah, no! already doth the hapless lot
Of Atlas, my own brother, torture me.
He on o'erladen shoulders in the west
Bears up the pillars of the Earth and Heaven.

So also have I seen, and pitying seen,
Him, the earthborn, impetuous Typhos, deep
Beneath Sicilian caverns sent to dwell.
Dire, with his hundred crests, his aspect was,
Portentous; and though now o'erthrown, he once,
Hissing forth slaughter from his monstrous jaws,
Faced all the embattled Gods, while from his eyes
Gorgonlike lights came flashing, as he stood
In act to storm the sovereignty of Heaven!
But him the ever-wakeful bolt of Zeus,
With thunder swooping, in a blast of flame,
Struck down astonied at the very height
Of his proud vauntings; stricken to the heart,
Charred, blasted, in his ruined strength he fell.
Now, prostrate, powerless, near the narrow seas,
Crushed 'neath the roots of Etna, lieth he;
And o'er him upon high Hephaistos sits
Where ring his glowing forges; thence one day
Shall break forth flaming torrents to devour
The smooth expanse of fruitful Sicily.
Such rage, though calcined by the bolts of Zeus,
The Titan still hath force to vomit forth
In hot insatiate floods of fiery surge.
But thou no novice art, nor need hast aught

That I should teach thee; save thyself, as well
Thou knowest how to do it; meanwhile I
Will drain my fate down to the dregs, till Zeus
Of his own will grow placable once more.

   Ocean. Knowest thou not, Prometheus, that apt
       words
Minister healing to a mind diseased?

   Prom. Aye, soothe a heart in season, but seek not
To lower a proud will in its own despite.

   Ocean. Doth evil, as of right, fall on the man
Who dares be zealous for the right? Tell me!

   Prom. On fussiness and feather-headed folly!

   Ocean. Let me seem sick of that complaint!
       Give me
Wisdom, for choice, without the look of it.

   Prom. Appearances lay that at my own door!

   Ocean. You bid me plainly get me home again.

   Prom. Aye, for I fear this dirge of thine for me
Should cast thee in disfavour.

   Ocean.   What, with him
Who sits upon the seat of power?

   Prom.   Take care
How you offend him.

   Ocean.   Thy calamities

Will teach me that.

Prom. Away, then ; get you home ;
And, mind, hold fast to that last sentiment.

Ocean. You could not read that to a readier mind.
The wings of this four-footed bird of mine
Fret Heaven's sleek ways already ; fain is he
To curl his knees on his own stable floor.

[*Exit Oceanus.*

Chorus.

1st Strophé. I do bewail thy ruinous plight,
Mine eyes grow tender at the sight,
And from their founts adown my face
In dewy rills the teardrops race.
All pitilessly thus doth Zeus
Of will-made law make lawless use,
Loving to flaunt his arrogant sway
Over the Gods of yesterday.

1st Antistrophé. The broad earth sends a moaning
    cry
To see thee and thy brethren lie,
And weeps for the long-honoured grace,
And olden grandeur of thy race.

And tribes of men, who for a home
O'er Asia's holy borders roam,
Make answer to thee, moan for moan,
In pangs responsive to thine own.

2nd Strophé. And all that warlike maiden host
Who dwell within the Colchian coast,
And Scythians, whose lone company
Haunteth the far Mæotian sea;

2nd Antistrophé. And all Arabia's martial flower,
Who hold the high Caucasian tower,
Dread hordes, who shout for joy to hear
The clash of the sharp-pointed spear.

3rd Strophé. But one God outraged have I known
By tortures equal to thine own;
The matchless Atlas, underground,
In adamantine shackles bound,
Earth's mighty mass and Heaven's wide spheres
On his unresting shoulder rears.

3rd Antistrophé. And to lament such infamy
The lashing sea-deeps rave and cry;

Gulph falls on gulph with answering groan,
Dark Hades sends a half-heard moan,
And sacred river-sources sigh
And shiver with thine agony.

Prom. 'Tis not from pride or stubbornness of soul
That I am silent; thought gnaws at my heart
To find myself maltreated thus: and yet,
To whose hand do these new Gods owe their honours,
If not to mine? But why say aught of this?
Speaking I should but speak to those who know.
But let me tell you how I found mankind
Blind miserable souls, and 'stablished them
In reason and the mastery of mind.
—I say not this to the reproach of man,
'Tis but to start the tale of my good-will.—
For seeing, till that day they had not seen,
Nor hearing heard, but like the shadowy forms
That people dreams, at random all their time
Had mingled all things heedlessly. They built
No sunny homes of brick in the bright air;
No wood they wrought; but in the sunless rifts

Of caverns burrowing, like windblown ants,
They dwelt; nor had they signs whereby to fix
Winter, or flowery Spring, or fruitful Summer;
But all they did was done without a mind;
Until I showed to them the mysteries
Of stars, and of their rising and decline.
And numbers too, the master science of all,
And writing I bestowed; and memory,
Mother of Muses, worker of all arts;
And was the first to make wild animals
Obedient to the yoke, that they might grow
Man's partners and his substitutes in toil.
And to the chariot first I led the horse,
Beneath my hand grown tolerant of the rein,
To make man's pride and luxury; and none
Ere me the canvas pinions of a ship
Sent voyaging; such new contrivances,
To mitigate their lot, did I achieve,
To mine own cost, for mortals, but, alas!
I find none now to serve myself withal.

 Chor. Thy miseries and shame have wildered
   thee;
And like some poor physician fallen ill,
Thou hast lost heart, and knowest not how to find

What drug may be specific of thy cure.
Prom. Oh, hear me out, and thou shalt wonder
 more
At all the arts and crafts that I contrived.
This chief of all ; in sickness if they fell,
They knew no remedy, no healing food,
Unguent, or beverage, but all for lack
Of pharmacy they pined away, till I
Taught them the compound of assuaging cures,
And rescue from all manner of disease.
Then, many a mode of prophecy I ordered,
And divination ; and the first was I
To pluck the waking truths out of a dream,
And from wild cries and sounds mysterious
Catch and unravel omens intricate.
So, from the flight of crooked-taloned birds,
Classing the boders both of good and ill,
I did determine wayside auguries,
And teach their habits, and their natural hates,
Loves, and gregarious affinities.
Nay more, I taught the semblance and intent
Of the smooth entrail, and the tint that makes
A victim pleasant to the Gods, and all
The veinèd symmetry of gall and liver.

And limbs o'erlain with fat; and the long chine
How they should burn; and so I led mankind
Through the hard maze of sacrificial art,
And fiery tokens all till then obscure.
All this I did, and who but I may claim
For man the buried treasures of the earth
To have exhumed, bronze, iron, silver, gold?
No one; vain boast apart, I know this well.
In one short word let me assure thee then,
Man hath learned all things from Prometheus.

Chor. Well;
Carry not over far this championship,
Careless of thine own fortunes; I hope still
To see thee, when thou hast thrown off these bonds,
Not one whit less in might than Zeus himself.

Prom. Fate, that brings all things to their purposed ends,
Is not thus shaped for me. I shall escape,
But after infinite suffering and woe.
Skill is far weaker than Necessity.

Chor. Who sways the rudder of Necessity?

Prom. The triple-visaged Fates and mindful Furies.

Chor. Is Zeus himself then weaker than all these?

Prom. Aye, even he cannot avoid his doom.

Chor. What doom is his except to reign for ever?

Prom. Ask me not this, no prayer could win my answer.

Chor. Is there then some dread thing that thou thus veilest?

Prom. Turn to some other topic, 'tis not yet
The time to talk of this, for this must be
Most sedulously hid, and in the hiding
Lies my escape from shameful bonds and pain.

Chorus.

1*st Strophé.* Oh, may Zeus never set
The mighty force he wields athwart my will,
And may I never in my turn forget
    Due homage to fulfil,
    Whene'er the victim bleeds
Beside our Father's quenchless waterways
At pious feasts; but may my words and deeds
    Mindfully shape my days.

2*nd Strophé.* Sweet 'twere to wreathe the chain
Of life's long span with hopes that fortify,
And sweet the heart to pamper in a train
    Of light and gaiety!
    Yet do I shudder here

At thee ground down by myriad agonies
Because for Zeus thou hadst no fitting fear
    And Man didst overprize.

   1st Antistrophé. How graceless is thy grace!
Tell me, my friend, what solace or what aid
Comes of these creatures of a day, this race
    Whose being is a shade,
    Such as a dream may weave;
Blind phantom brood, and bondsmen unto gloom,
To whom, without remission or reprieve,
    Zeus doth decree their doom!

   2nd Antistrophé. These words, these measures
    grow
From gazing on thy misery and pain,
And I, alas! have learned them of thy woe;
    Far other was the strain
    In which our voices vied
Merrily round thy bath and bridal-bed,
Whereto, well-dowered, our sister and thy bride,
    Hesione, we led.

    Enter Io *loq.*
What land is this? And you, what race are ye?

Whom do I see thus bridled here in stone,
Outstretched, a prey to storms and winter? What
The crimes under whose penalties thou diest?
Tell me the land which I, the weary one,
Have wandered to. Alas, alas, poor wretch!
Once more the gadfly's venom stingeth me!
Earth, take away this phantom of thy son,
Argos, the herdsman, myriad-eyed! I see him;
He haunts me ever with his crafty gaze;
He whom the earth, dead though he be, can hide
    not.
He cometh up to chase me, woe is me!
He makes me wander fasting by the shore
Along the sands that border it, the while
The waxy marsh-reeds that he pipes upon
Drone out their drowsy measures!
Alas! Oh, whither tend these wanderings?
Ah, say, thou son of Kronos, for what fault
Hast thou thus harnessed me to tortures? Why
Goad me to madness with this stinging terror?
Blast me with flames; bid the earth bury me;
Or to the monsters of the ocean deeps
Fling me for food!
Grudge me not some such boon of death, O King!

Enough, enough of bootless wanderings
That strip me e'en to nakedness, but show
Neither relief nor issue.
[*To Prometheus.*]   Dost thou hear
The crying of the wretched heifer-maid?

 Prom. How should I not, daughter of Inachus,
Spurred by the gadfly's poison? Thou, whose love
The heart of Zeus infected, and whom now
The hate of Heré goadeth on to scour
The earth round in immeasurable travel.

 Io. Ah, how hast thou let fall my father's name?
Tell me, me wretched, who thou art, who thus,
Thyself a sufferer, hast described aright
Me and my sufferings, and the heaven-sent pest
That tears, and wears, and mars, and maddens me!
'Tis true; I have been driven to scour the earth
Under the spells of Heré's angry will,
In violence, in famine, and in shame.
Alas, alas! of all ill-fated ones
Whose is there that may match my misery?
Oh say, oh say, what have I yet to bear?
If any means or antidote may be
Within thy range of knowledge, tell it me;

Oh tell, oh tell the wretched outcast maid.

Prom. Aye, I will tell thee all that thou wouldst know;
Weaving no riddles, but in simple words
Such as a friendly mouth should ope to utter.
I am Prometheus, who dowered man with fire.

Io. O thou, who wast made manifest to work
The general redemption of mankind,
Prometheus, O unhappy one, I would know
What is the cause or crime thou sufferest for.

Prom. I have but just now ceased my threnody.

Io. Well then, accord another boon to me.

Prom. Ask what thou wilt, and I will tell it to thee.

Io. Then say, who strapped thee to this rocky cleft?

Prom. Zeus of design, Hephaistos by his hand.

Io. And what the errors thou dost expiate?

Prom. Thus far is far enough, I say no more.

Io. Well, tell me then, what time shall set a term
To these my miserable wanderings?

Prom. 'Twere better for thee not to know these things.

Io. Withhold not from me what I have to bear.
Prom. It is not that I grudge the boon to thee!
Io. Why hesitate then thus to tell me all?
Prom. 'Tis not ill will; I would not vex thy soul.
Io. Dismiss all fear for me, I yearn to hear.
Prom. So keen thy wish that I will speak. So listen.
Chor. Not yet, give me my meed of pleasure too;
Let us first hear the story of her ill;
Let her recount her ruinous mishaps,
Then be it thine her future to unfold.
Prom. Io, 'tis meet thou favour them thus far,
The rather that they are thy father's sisters.
Also, to weep, and to bewail our lot
With those whose tears stand ready to be drawn,
Is worth its cost of effort or of time.
Io. I know not how to question what you say;
So shall ye hear the plain tale ye desire.
And yet I weep for very shame to tell
How the wild hurricane of heavenly wrath
Played havoc with my body, woe is me!
For soft seducing voices of the night

Would haunt my virgin chamber: "Happy maid,
Why dost thou hold thyself aloof," they said,
"Thou who may'st mate thyself so high? 'Tis Zeus
Who burning with the bolt of love's desire
Would share its flames with thee. Oh then, my child,
Spurn not the couch of Zeus; but hie thee forth,
To Lerné's deep and grassy meads, and there
Amid the flocks and homesteads of thy sire
Comfort the eyes divine that ache for thee."
Night after night was I bestead by dreams
Until I dared to tell them to my sire.
But he to Pytho and Dodona sent
Full many a holy man, that he might learn
By word or deed to satisfy the Gods.
But such returned upon us bringing back
Phrases of doubt and varying import,
Dark, meaningless, and all obscurely framed.
Till at the last there came to Inachus
One peremptory mandate answering clear,
That bade him drive me from my home and country,
Outcast to wander to earth's utmost bounds.

This should he fail to do, the fire-faced bolt
Of Zeus should fall and extirpate his house.
Cowed by these utterances of Loxias,
Full loth on me full loth my father shut
His doors, and outcast drave me from my home.
The will divine, like an o'ermastering curb,
Compelled him to the deed. Then straightway came
On me distortion of my form, and mind
Distraught; then bitten by the keen-fanged fly,
And crested as you see, with maddened bounds
I rushed to the sweet water of Kerchneia
And to the springs of Lerné; this my course
Argos, the earthborn herdsman, watched with mood
Untempered, changeless, while his hundred eyes
Glared on my track; him did a doom unlooked for,
Sudden, destroy; but I, envenomed still,
Am scourged by lash divine from land to land.
Ye hear my past.
[*To Prometheus.*]   If thou hast aught to tell,
Of what remains to bear, oh! speak; soothe not
My soul with pitying falsehood; I should count
Such words but added sickness and worse shame.

   Chor. Forbear; I never dreamed words strange
      as these

Would reach mine ear,
Or that my soul would freeze,
Chilled through with two-edged fear,
In face of shame, wrongs, horror, and despair,
As dread to look on as to bear.
O Fate, Fate, Fate,
I shudder as I gaze on Io and her state!
   Prom. Too soon ye wail and fill your souls with fear;
Wait ye awhile, and hear the residue.
   Chor. Speak then; 'tis comfort to the sick to know
The limit of the pains they must endure.
   Prom. Lightly ye gained what ye first asked of me,
For ye would hear from her own lips the tale
Of her own trouble; hear ye now what yet
At Heré's hands the damsel shall endure.
Thou too, O child of Inachus, my words
Lay to thine heart; so shalt thou learn the term
Of this thy travel. When thou leavest me,
Turn towards the sunrise, and the ploughless tracts
Shall bring thee to the wandering Scythians,

Who, with far-ranging bows equipped, on wheels
Of well-turned wains their wattled homes suspend.
Approach them not, but pass beyond their land,
And skirt the resonant margin of the sea.
Thence to the left dwell those whom thou must shun,
The iron-working Chalybes, for rude
Are they, and unto strangers perilous.
So, to the river, not unaptly named
The proud, o'erbearing river, shalt thou come,
But not essay to cross him there, thy foot
Shall find no ford in him before thou win
The heights of overtopping Caucasus.
There doth the stream disgorge his violence
Sheer from the mountain's brow: thou must o'er-climb
The very crests that neighbour with the stars,
And take the southern pass to find the host
Of man-abominating Amazons;
They who one day along Thermodon's banks
Shall on the plains of Themiscyra dwell,
Where, by the rough jaws of the Pontic sea,
Inhospitable Salmydessus lies,
A cruel stepmother to fleets and men.

These with much zeal shall speed thee on thy way.
And thus to the Cimmerian Chersonese,
Up to the gorge that makes the narrow gate
Of the great Lake, shalt thou arrive ; therefrom
With heart unflinching dare to plunge, and stem
The floods of the Mæotian strait ; for know
The fame of that thy passage shall survive
Upon the tongues of men, and Bosphoros
Shall thence be called the heifer-bearing stream.
So from the plains of Europe shalt thou gain
The continent of Asia.
[*To the Chorus.*]   Well, what think ye?
Is not the tyrant of the Gods alike
High-handed everywhere ? See ye not how,
Baulked of his lust with this young mortal, he
Hath cast on her this curse of wandering ?
[*To Io.*] Bitter the chance, O damsel, that hath
    dowered thee
With such a suitor : what thou hast just heard
Is but the prelude to thy history.

  Io. Alas, alas, then, woe is me !

  Prom. What ? Moans and cries afresh ! What
    wilt thou do
When thou shalt learn thy residue of ill ?

Chor. What is there more of ill to tell her then?
Prom. A sea, a wintry sea, of bane and woe!
Io. If this be so, what profit is my life?
Why not at once fling myself headlong down
From these wild rocks, and on the plain beneath
Find my release from suffering? 'Twere better
Thus to die once, at once, than linger out
The full tale of my days in agony!
Prom. How wouldst thou fail to bear my trials!
    Me
To whom no death is fated! Death indeed
Were a release; but now to me no end
Lieth in sight till Zeus shall fall from power.
Io. What sayest thou? Shall Zeus then fall from
    power?
Prom. I ween thou wouldst rejoice o'er that
    mischance.
Io. And why not, seeing how I suffer through
    him?
Prom. Then take it as a fact foreheard by thee.
Io. And who is he shall spoil him of his sceptre?
Prom. 'Tis he himself of his own fatuous will.
Io. But tell me how, if no harm be in telling.
Prom. Of ruinous wedlock will the mischief come.

Io. Heavenly, or earthly? Tell us, if thou mayest.

Prom. Why ask me which? I may not tell thee which.

Io. Will then his wife eject him from his throne?

Prom. Aye, she will bear a son too strong for him.

Io. And is there naught that can divert this doom?

Prom. Naught, none save I, set free from these my bonds.

Io. But who could free thee in despite of Zeus?

Prom. It is decreed; one of thy seed shall do it.

Io. How sayest thou? Shall son of mine release thee?

Prom. He who is born the thirteenth of thy line.

Io. I find it hard to piece thy prophecy.

Prom. Leave it and thine own lot alike unlearned.

Io. Thou wilt not now withdraw thy proffered boon?

Prom. I offer thee a choice of narratives.

Io. First tell me what they are, then let me choose.

Prom. I will; choose either that I tell thee all
That thou hast yet to undergo, or else
Divulge the name of my deliverer.

Chor. Why not tell one to her, and one to me,
And so slight neither? Let her know the rest
Of all her wanderings, and me the name
Of thy deliverer; I yearn to hear it.

Prom. Since ye insist, I will not say ye nay,
But all which ye are suppliants for reveal.
And, Io, first to thee will I set forth
Thy course, driven, as it were, of many waves;
Which grave upon the tablets of thy mind.
When thou hast crossed the strait that makes the
    bounds
Of the two continents, take thou thy road
Up the sun-trodden pathways of the East;
So shalt thou cross a sounding sea, and reach
Cisthene, and the plains Gorgonian;
There dwell the Phorcides, three dames, swan-
    formed,
Ancient of days, one eye, one tooth, alone
Their joint possession, upon whom the sun
Turns not his rays, nor hers the nightly moon.
And near them do their wingèd sisters dwell,
The Gorgons three, snake-haired, abhorred of men,
Whom nothing mortal may behold and live.
Garrison thou thy soul with this last hint!

Now of another sight intolerable
Must thou beware, the Gryphons, who for Zeus,
Mute and sharp-fanged as ban-dogs, are on guard.
And that one-eyed equestrian array
Of Arimaspians, who cluster round
The golden-sanded streams and fords of Plutus.
Approach them not, but seek by distant ways
That swarthy race who near the dayspring dwell,
Hard by the river of the Æthiops.
Steal up its banks to that broad cataract
Where from the Bybline mountain Nilus pours
His sacred and salubrious waters; he
Shall guide thee, Io, to the destined soil,
Triangular, of Nile, whereon at length
Thou and thy seed shall found your distant
    homes.
And now, if I have faltered, or if aught
Seem hard to trace, reduplicate your quest,
And learn all thoroughly, for, as thou seest,
I have more leisure than I value here.

  Chor. If aught remain omitted or untold
Of all her sad and cruel wanderings,
Tell; but, if all be told, thou dost bethink thee
Of that same boon I craved of thee anon?

Prom. Of her long travel she hath learned the
    term ;
But yet, lest she should deem what she hath heard
An idle tale, I will rehearse to her
Her dire experience hitherwards, and so
Give voucher for my power to prophesy.
I may pass o'er the mass of incident,
And touch the closing stages of thy course.
So ; having reached to the Molossian plains
And ridgy-backed Dodona, where are found
The seats and oracle of Thesprotian Zeus,
And that incredible portent above all,
The Talking Oaks, 'twas no uncertain voice
Hailed thee with honour as the bride of Zeus—
I know not if the style found favour with thee—
Thence, goaded by the gadfly, didst thou race
Along the margin of the sea, and reached
Rhea's great gulph, whence now thou urgest on
The stormy flux and reflux of thy way.
And, for a sign that my presaging soul
Transcends the mere presentments of the past,
Know thou that bay of ocean shall from thee
Be called of all men the Ionian gulph,
In memory of thy passage. What remains

I tell to you in common, to the track
Returning of my earlier history.
On that last cape, where at his very mouth
The silt of Nilus ceases, stands a city,
Canopus called ; there 'tis that Zeus at last
By touch, and touch alone, of soothing hand
Shall once again restore thee to thyself.
And there, from that engendering touch so named,
Shalt thou bring forth the dark-skinned Epaphos,
Who shall enjoy the wealth of all that land
Which the broad waters of the Nile o'erflow.
Thence, of the generation fifth from him,
A group of fifty virgins shall take flight
Unwillingly to Argos, to elude
Wedlock too close akin ; whose suitor cousins
Shall after them, as falcons after doves,
Empassioned rush, in chase of marriages
That are no proper quarry, and of brides
Against whose capture Heaven shall set itself.
Their bodies shall Pelasgic earth receive,
Slain by the midnight daring of their wives ;
For, bathing in his throat the two-edged sword,
Shall each bereave her husband of his life.
To such love-doom come all mine enemies !

One only, under passion's witchery,
Shall blunt her will and spare her bedfellow,
Of two ills choosing rather to be called
Feeble of heart than murderess ; but she
In Argos shall bring forth a race of kings—
O'erlong it were to tell her story out—
But of her seed a hero shall be born,
A far-famed archer, who from these my pains
Shall free me ; such a weird mine ancient mother,
Themis the Titanid, did read for me.
But how, and where, that too 'twere long to tell,
And thou wouldst nothing gain in hearing it.

 Io. Alas ! alas ! ah me ! ah me !
Once more the spasm of agony, once more
Soul-piercing frenzies scorch me, and once more
That barb no fire e'er forged, the gadfly's sting,
Envenoms me ; my heart knocks at my ribs
For very terror ; on a furious blast
Of madness am I whirled away ; mine eyes
Roll wildly ; and my random tongue, broke loose,
With turbid words doth hurl itself in vain
Against the surf of my calamity ! [*Exit Io.*

Chorus.

1st Strophé. Ah, wise, ah, surely wise, was he
Who was the first to think and say,
"Let not thy random fancy stray,
But wed thee in thine own degree,
Thou toiler of a mean estate,
Nor from the pampered ones of earth,
Nor among those of lordly birth
Seek for thy mate."

1st Antistrophé. Never, ye Fates, may your dread
    eyes
Behold me as the bedfellow
Of Zeus, nor I be forced to go
To any bridegroom of the skies.
I tremble gazing on the plight
Of Io, matchless maiden, hurled
In tortured exile through the world,
By Heré's spite.

2nd Strophé. For me I shall not fear to find
A kindly match among my kind,
But may no loftier deity
Cast love's imperious glance on me!

2nd Antistrophé. O power of fight all fight that
      stays,
That cleaves a path through pathless ways,
How could I hope to foil or flee,
If Zeus should harbour thought of me?

Prom. And yet shall he, imperious though he be,
Be humbled by this very means of marriage!
A plotted marriage from his sovereign seat
Shall hurl him out of sight; and so the curse
Shall be accomplished which his father Kronos
Launched as he fell from his primæval throne.
Nor is there one among the Gods, save I,
Who can avoid this ruin for him; I
Know both the end and means. So, for a while
Let him sit there secure, on his high thunders
Reliant, brandishing his fiery bolts.
For nothing shall avail him that he fall not,
Dishonoured, in a fall unsufferable.
So dread a foeman doth he for himself
Prepare, a portent of resistless power,
Who shall find flames the lightning to outlighten,
A sound the blare of thunder to outblare,
And force to shiver that earth-shaking pest,

Poseidon's triple spear; and then shall Zeus,
Thus stumbling into ruin, learn by proof
The distance 'twixt the tyrant and the slave!
  Chor. Is not thy wish the parent to thy words?
  Prom. I speak of what shall be and what I wish.
  Chor. And must we then expect to see Zeus serve?
  Prom. Aye, with a neck more overbowed than mine.
  Chor. Hast thou no fear in flinging forth such words?
  Prom. What need I fear who am not doomed to die?
  Chor. But he may put thee to some greater trial.
  Prom. Let him; I have looked forth on everything.
  Chor. They are the wise who worship Adrastea.
  Prom. Worship ye, pray ye, truckle ye to the strong!
To me Zeus is of less account than nothing.
Let him for his brief span work all his will,
And play the tyrant; 'twill not be for long.
But no more now; for here I see the slave,

The running lacquey of his new-made lord,
Who doth his errands; he without a doubt
Hath come to tell us of some fresh resolve.

Enter HERMES *loq.*

Master of craft, bitterly over-bitter
Sinner against the Gods, thou furnisher
Of high prerogatives to man, fire-filcher,
A word with thee! The Father ordereth thee
To say what are these vaunted nuptials
Thou pratest of, by which he is to fall
From sovereignty. No riddles, so it please thee;
But speak out, all and everything; I want
No second journey cast on me; besides,
That would not be the way to soften Zeus.

Prom. Full of solemnity and insolence
Thy speech, as fits the underling of the Gods!
Your rule is young, ye upstarts, yet ye think
Ye dwell in towers that none can trouble. What?
Have I not seen two dynasties fall therefrom?
Aye, and a third shall I behold hurled out
With greater speed and shame than either of these.
I trust I do not seem to cringe or cower
Before these new divinities; for much,

Aye, wholly, do I lack the feeling. Thou,
By the same way thou camest, get thee back!
Thou shalt learn naught of what thou askest me.

Herm. By just such headstrong wilfulness as this
It is that thou hast landed thyself here.

Prom. I would not barter this my wretchedness,
Know well, for that same servitude of thine.
Better to be a bondsman to this rock
Than to be born the come-and-go of Zeus.
I hold affront fair pay for insolence.

Herm. Thou seem'st to revel in thy present state.

Prom. Revel! I would I saw mine enemies
Indulged with such a revel! Thee among them.

Herm. But why me too? With what canst thou charge me?

Prom. I, in one word, hate the whole pack of Gods,
Whom I did well for, and who ill-treat me.

Herm. 'Tis clear thou'rt maddened in no small degree.

Prom. Let me be mad, if to hate foes be madness.

Herm. Thou'dst be unbearable if prosperous.

Prom. Alas!

Herm. That is a word Zeus knoweth not.
Prom. Ah! we learn all things as time groweth old.
Herm. But thou hast hardly learned discretion yet.
Prom. Or else I should not talk to underlings.
Herm. It seems thou'lt not tell what the Father asks.
Prom. Forsooth I am so deeply in his debt!
Herm. Thou chidest me as though I were a boy.
Prom. Art not a boy? Aye, duller than a boy,
For dreaming I should tell thee anything!
There is no torture, no device, whereby
Zeus could impel me to disclose this thing,
Unless he first released me from these bonds.
Let him then blast me with his fiery bolts,
Confound the air with snowdrifts, and make rock
The earth with subterranean thunders: me
He shall not bend to tell him by what hand
It is decreed that he shall fall from power.
Herm. Think now, will all this work thee any aid?
Prom. All this hath been presaged and pre-resolved.

Herm. Nay, brook, thou madman, brook at last to set
A truer value on thy present pains.
Prom. As waves a rock, thy vain advice doth fret me.
Harbour no fancy that for dread of Zeus
I shall turn womanish, and like a woman
Lift hands, and pray my most detested foe
To let me loose; I wholly lack the will.
Herm. Much have I said, but all, it seems, in vain ;
No prayers will soften or subdue thy soul ;
And as a horse unbroken champs his bit,
And strains and struggles with the reins, so thou.
Yet weak the sophistry that hardeneth thee ;
For stubbornness, by wisdom all unbacked,
Standing alone, is less than nothing worth.
Bethink thee, if my words persuade thee not,
What an inevitable storm and surge
Of evils shall assail thee ; first the Father
With thunders and the lightning shaft shall rend
This rocky gorge asunder, and immure
Thy body shrouded in its stony arms ;
Then, after a long lapse of time fulfilled,

Back shalt thou rise to light; from which time forth
The wingèd hound of Zeus, the bloody eagle,
Thy mangled trunk shall furiously tear,
And stay, a late, unbidden banqueter,
To gorge on thy dark liver. Of this plague
Look for no close; unless some God incline
To take up the succession to thy pain,
Descend to rayless Hades, and be pent
Amid the murky deeps of Tartarus.
Think on all this; it is no idle threat,
But told thee in all earnestness, for Zeus
Lets not his mouth outrun itself, but will
Fulfil his every word. Do thou then look
And ponder, nor esteem thy stubbornness
As better than good counsel and resolve.

   Chor. To us it seems that Hermes' words have
      been
Not out of season; he hath bade thee seek
Good counsels, and to lay recusance down.
It is a scandal for the wise to sin
Against the wisdom that is in them. Yield!

   Prom. I knew this message coming, ere it came;
    In vain his wordy task doth he fulfil;

I am the foe of Zeus, and feel no shame
   To suffer torture at my foeman's will.
      Let him then hurl at his desire
         His clustered lightning's two-edged fire,
And let the wrestling thunder rave and tear
With clatter of mad winds the writhing air.

And may the fury of the rending blast
   The deep foundations of the earth upraise,
And ocean's billows in confusion cast
   Their violent surge among the starry ways.
      Then may he headlong to the deep
         Of Tartarus my body sweep,
On Fate's resistless eddies whirled away;
I am content, he hath no power to slay.

   Herm. To hearken to him is to hear
A madman's ravings, word and will;
How falls it short of madness sheer
In such a plight to struggle still?
For you, who came to mourn and bear
Of his calamities a share,
To you, begone at once, I say,
And quit this perilous neighbourhood,

Lest the dread bellow of thunder should
Scare all your wits away!

Chor. 'Twere well that thy persuasion took
Some other form of greater grace,
For scarcely know I how to brook
These promptings false to time and place.
Why dost thou bid me to be base?
I tell thee I am here to bear
Whatever must be borne, and face
All things with him who hangeth there.
Traitors have I been taught to hate,
And faithful to my teaching, I
Loathe treason as a foul estate,
Fouler than foulest malady.

Herm. Remember what my words have been;
Nor for your troubles Fortune blame,
Nor ever plead that unforeseen
From Zeus your plunge to ruin came;
Ye foreknew all, nor unawares,
Nor suddenly, your folly set
And wove around yourselves the snares
Of woe's unfathomable net. [*Exit Hermes.*

Prom. The threat hath taken form, the earth doth quake,
Up from her depths the thunder's echo roars,
In mighty wreaths the lightnings blaze and break,
And spinning coils of dust the whirlwind soars.

The winds 'gainst one another dash,
And air and sea commingled clash;
So vast the stroke and blast of fear
Striking from Zeus that stalketh here.

O, my majestic mother, Earth, and thou,
Æther, whose whirling course doth bear to all
The common light of Heaven, be witness now
How undeserved on me these sufferings fall!

THE YEAR.

WE keep our company with thoughts that would sadden
    The Year itself, were the Year not sad ;
Nor could Earth change her vesture so as to gladden
    Our souls, or chill them, however clad.

For we are stamped with memories of a branding
    Too deep and sure for her suns to fade,
Tincts upon loss by sorrow wrought, and withstanding
    Time's wistful proffer of chastened shade.

Then robe thyself with Autumn, Earth, or with Summer,
    Winter, or Spring, they shall be as one ;
Our hearts shall find for each, as for a new comer,
    A contrast still or an undertone.

CHISWICK PRESS:—CHARLES WHITTINGHAM AND CO.
TOOKS COURT, CHANCERY LANE, LONDON.

www.ingramcontent.com/pod-product-compliance
Lightning Source LLC
Chambersburg PA
CBHW020255170426
43202CB00008B/381